A DICTIONARY OF NEW TESTAMENT GREEK SYNONYMS

A DICTIONARY OF NEW TESTAMENT GREEK SYNONYMS

with indexes to
Bauer's
GREEK-ENGLISH LEXICON
and Brown's
DICTIONARY OF
NEW TESTAMENT THEOLOGY

GEORGE RICKER BERRY

**ZONDERVAN
PUBLISHING HOUSE** OF THE ZONDERVAN CORPORATION
GRAND RAPIDS, MICHIGAN 49506

A Dictionary of New Testament Greek Synonyms
Copyright © 1979 by the Zondervan Corporation
Grand Rapids, Michigan

Library of Congress Cataloging in Publication Data

Berry, George Ricker, 1865-1945.
  A dictionary of New Testament Greek synonyms.

  Based in part on the author's A new Greek-English lexicon to the New Testament and on R. C. Trench's Synonyms of the New Testament.
  Includes index.
  1. Greek language, Biblical—Synonyms and antonyms.
  2. Greek language, Biblical—Dictionaries—Enlgish.
  I. Berry, George Ricker, 1865-1945. A new Greek-English lexicon to the New Testament.   II. Trench, Richard Chenevix, abp. of Dublin, 1807-1886. Synonyms of the New Testament.   III. Title.

ISBN 0-310-21161-1

All rights reserved. No part of this publication may be reproduced in any form or by any means without the prior permission of the copyright owner.

Printed in the United States of America

83   84   85   86   87   88 — 10   9   8   7   6   5   4   3

Contents

Preface to the New Edition / 7
Preface to the First Edition / 9

PART 1
Synonym Distinctions / 13

PART 2
Index to Synonym Distinctions / 43

PART 3
Synonym Groupings With Index to Bauer's
Greek-English Lexicon / 49

PART 4
Synonym List With Index to Brown's
Dictionary of New Testament Theology / 79

Preface to the New Edition

Berry's synonym studies were originally part of his book *A New Greek-English Lexicon to the New Testament,* published by Wilcox & Follett in 1897. This volume contained a 110-page lexicon plus a 21-page excursus on various synonyms. Although the lexicon gave definitions of words, as most language dictionaries do, it also presented information about 161 synonyms (with an additional 132 in the excursus). Unfortunately, the synonym material from both the lexicon and the excursus has not been greatly used because these two portions have appeared for a number of years now as appendixes in Berry's *Interlinear Greek-English New Testament.* This neglect has been particularly true of the synonym analysis in the lexicon, since this analysis can be found only by using the book's index. The present edition includes not only Berry's excursus (Part 1) but also all the synonym discussions from the lexicon, with the latter material being in both Part 1: Synonym Distinctions and Part 3: Synonym Groupings With Index to Bauer's *Greek English Lexicon.*

Without a doubt, the classic book on synonyms is R. C. Trench's *Synonyms of the New Testament.* Trench discussed 323 synonyms and suggested 244 more in the preface to his eighth edition, but his extensive use of Latin has rendered many parts of his work unintelligible to most Bible students today. Although Berry used Trench and others (see footnote on page10), he avoided lengthy treatises; indeed, his studies of 293 synonyms are marked by clarity and conciseness. In Trench's and Berry's books, most of the major synonyms and many of the minor ones are either defined or grouped; so all the synonym listings from Trench's preface and text have been combined with those in Berry's lexicon and excursus to produce 574 synonym groupings. All these synonym groupings have been indexed to the recently released second English edition of Walter Bauer's *Greek-English Lexicon of the New Testament,* which supplies bibliographical data and extrabiblical references necessary for synonym differentiations.

There have been a number of word-study books published

subsequent to both Trench's and Berry's volumes, the most notable being Kittel and Friedrich's *Theological Dictionary of the New Testament* and Brown's *New International Dictionary of New Testament Theology*. Neither of these works has dealt solely with synonyms, but both have pointed out the implications, connotations, and applications of some word meanings and thus have provided a base for distinguishing certain synonyms. Because Brown's 3-volume set is more concise and up-to-date than Kittel and Friedrich's 10-volume set, the total synonym list from both Trench and Berry has been indexed to the former, though the diligent student will want to consult the 10-volume work. In fact, such a student can add to Trench's and Berry's lists by examining the entries in recent word-study books.

In light of the need for a new book devoted solely to New Testament synonyms, it is hoped that the present volume will be a catalyst to scholars and, in the process, will help the Bible student to appreciate the Swiftian phrase—"proper words in proper places."

The Publisher

Preface to the First Edition

A *careful* discrimination between synonyms in the study of any language is a matter of the utmost importance, and also consequently of considerable difficulty. But there are some considerations which make a treatment of the synonyms of the New Testament especially difficult and especially necessary. The Greek language in classical times was one which was admirably adapted for expressing fine shades of meaning, and therefore one which abounded in synonyms. In later Greek, outside of the New Testament, some of these distinctions were changed or modified. The writers of the New Testament were men of Semitic habits of thought and expression. They also had theological and ethical teachings to impart which were far more profound and spiritual than had been conveyed by the Greek language previous to that time. These and other facts affecting the New Testament Greek necessarily modify the meaning of many of the synonyms there used, in some cases effecting a complete transformation.

The object in the present treatment is to consider the New Testament usage. Hence, the distinctions of classical Greek are stated only so far as they are also found in New Testament usage, or are of importance for determining the latter. For a discrimination of the distinctive meanings of New Testament synonyms, three things must usually be considered:

First, the etymological meaning of the words;

Second, the relations in which the words are found in classical Greek;

Third, the relations in which they are found in New Testament Greek, the last being often the chief factor.

The use of the words in the Septuagint is also important, for their connection with the Hebrew words which they are used to translate often throws light on their meaning.

The discussions here given aim to be brief, but yet to outline clearly the important and fundamental differences of meaning. Some words which are often given in works on this subject have been omitted, for the reason that the definitions as given in the

Lexicon sufficiently indicate the important distinctions. There has been added, however, a consideration of some other words which are not so commonly included.

The chief works from which material and suggestions have been drawn are mentioned in the Introduction to the Lexicon.*

The reason is stated in the Introduction to the Lexicon why in some cases the same word is treated both in the synonyms of the Lexicon itself, and also in this place.† In every such instance the treatment here is to be regarded as supplementary to that in the Lexicon proper.

The synonyms here discussed do not belong exclusively nor chiefly to any one class of words. Both theological and non-theological terms are included. The aim has been to consider all the synonyms most likely to be confounded with one another, *i.e.*, all those most important, for practical use, to the average student of the New Testament.

---

*"Much material has been drawn from R. C. Trench, *Synonyms of the New Testament,* and from the New Testament Lexicons of Thayer and Cremer, as well as from the small ones of Green and Hickie."

†"The original plan in reference to Synonyms was to give in the Lexicon itself definitions of a few of the most important ones. After most of the Lexicon was in type, however, it was decided, in view of the importance of the subject, that a very helpful feature would be a special section devoted to Synonyms. This has accordingly been prepared. The result is, of course, that a few words already treated in the Lexicon have here been given a fuller treatment." [This duplication has been eliminated in the 1979 edition except for cases where the lexicon gave additional information.]

PART 1
Synonym Distinctions

Pages 13–33 are Berry's excursus on synonyms in the original book A New Greek-English Lexicon to the New Testament. *Pages 35–39 are from the lexicon itself.*

SYNONYM DISTINCTIONS

§ 1. Holy, sacred, pure.

ἱερός, ὅσιος, ἅγιος, ἁγνός, σεμνός.

None of these words in classical Greek has necessarily any moral significance. Those which now have such a meaning have developed it in Biblical Greek. ἱερός means *sacred*, implying some special relation to God, so that it may not be violated. It refers, however, to formal relation rather than to character. It designates an external relation, which ordinarily is not an internal relation as well. It is used to describe persons or things. This is the commonest word for *holy* in classical Greek, and expresses their usual conception of holiness, but it is rare in the N.T. because it fails to express the fullness of the N.T. conception. ὅσιος, used of persons or things, describes that which is in harmony with the divine constitution of the moral universe. Hence, it is that which is in accordance with the general and instinctively felt idea of right, "what is consecrated and sanctioned by universal law and consent" (Passow), rather than what is in accordance with any system of revealed truth. As contrary to ὅσιος, *i.e.*, as ἀνοσία, the Greeks regarded, *e.g.*, a marriage between brother and sister such as was common in Egypt, or the omission of the rites of sepulture in connection with a relative. ἅγιος has probably as its fundamental meaning *separation*, *i.e.*, from the world to God's service. If not the original meaning, this at any rate is a meaning early in use. This separation, however, is not chiefly external, it is rather a separation from evil and defilement. The moral signification of the word is therefore the prominent one. This word, rare and of neutral meaning in classical Greek, has been developed in meaning, so that it expresses the full N.T. conception of holiness as no other does. ἁγνός is probably related to ἅγιος. It means specifically *pure*. But this may be only in a ceremonial sense, or it may have a moral signification. It sometimes describes freedom from impurities of the flesh. σεμνός is that which inspires *reverence* or *awe*. In classical Greek it was often applied to the gods. But frequently it has the lower idea of that which is humanly venerable, or even refers simply to externals, as to that which is magnificent, grand, or impressive.

§ 2. Sin.

ἁμαρτία, ἁμάρτημα, ἀσέβεια, παρακοή, ἀνομία, παρανομία, παράβασις, παράπτωμα, ἀγνόημα, ἥττημα.

ἁμαρτία meant originally *the missing of a mark*. When applied to moral things the idea is similar, it is missing the true end of life, and so it is

SYNONYM DISTINCTIONS

used as a general term for *sin*. It means both the act of sinning and the result, the sin itself. ἁμάρτημα means only the sin itself, not the act, in its particular manifestations as separate deeds of disobedience to a divine law. ἀσέβεια is *ungodliness*, positive and active irreligion, a condition of direct opposition to God. παρακοή is strictly *failing to hear*, or hearing carelessly and inattentively. The sin is in this failure to hear when God speaks, and also in the active disobedience which ordinarily follows. ἀνομία is *lawlessness*, contempt of law, a condition or action not simply without law, as the etymology might indicate, but contrary to law. The law is usually by implication the Mosaic law. παρανομία occurs only once, 2 Pet. ii. 16, and is practically equivalent to ἀνομία. παράβασις is *transgression*, the passing beyond some assigned limit. It is the breaking of a distinctly recognized commandment. It consequently means more than ἁμαρτία. παράπτωμα is used in different senses, sometimes in a milder sense, denoting an error, a mistake, a fault; and sometimes meaning a trespass, a willful sin. ἀγνόημα occurs only once, Heb. ix. 7. It indicates *error*, sin which to a certain extent is the result of ignorance. ἥττημα denotes *being worsted, defeated*. In an ethical sense it means *a failure in duty, a fault*. — All these different words may occasionally but not usually be used simply to describe the same act from different points of view. The fundamental meanings of these words may well be summed up in the language of Trench: Sin "may be regarded as the missing of a mark or aim: it is then ἁμαρτία or ἁμάρτημα; the overpassing or transgressing of a line: it is then παράβασις; the disobedience to a voice: in which case it is παρακοή; the falling where one should have stood upright: this will be παράπτωμα; ignorance of what one ought to have known: this will be ἀγνόημα; diminishing of that which should have been rendered in full measure, which is ἥττημα; non-observance of a law, which is ἀνομία or παρανομία."

§ 3. Sincere.

ἁπλοῦς, ἀκέραιος, ἄκακος, ἄδολος.

ἁπλοῦς is literally *spread out without folds*, and hence means single, simple, without complexity of character and motive. In the N.T. this idea of simplicity is always favorable; in classical Greek the word is also occasionally used in an unfavorable sense, denoting foolish simplicity. ἀκέραιος also means *simple*, literally *free from any foreign admixture, unadulterated, free from disturbing elements*. ἄκακος in Heb. vii. 26 means one in whom exists absence of all evil, and so by implication the presence of all good. It passes

SYNONYM DISTINCTIONS

also through the merely negative meaning of absence of evil, found in S., to the unfavorable meaning of simple, easily deceived, credulous, which is found in Ro. xvi. 18. ἄδολος, occurring only in 1 Pet. ii. 2, means *sincere, unmixed, without guile.*

§ 4. Sins of the tongue.

μωρολογία, αἰσχρολογία, εὐτραπελία.

μωρολογία, used only once in the N.T., is *foolish talking*, but this in the Biblical sense of the word foolish, which implies that it is also sinful. It is conversation which is first insipid, then corrupt. It is random talk, which naturally reveals the vanity and sin of the heart. αἰσχρολογία, also used once, means any kind of disgraceful language, especially abuse of others. In classical Greek it sometimes means distinctively language which leads to lewdness. εὐτραπελία, occurring once, originally meant *versatility in conversation*. It acquires, however, an unfavorable meaning, since polished, refined conversation has a tendency to become evil in many ways. The word denotes, then, a subtle form of evil-speaking, sinful conversation without the coarseness which frequently accompanies it, but not without its malignity.

§ 5. Shame, disgrace.

αἰδώς, αἰσχύνη, ἐντροπή, (σωφροσύνη).

αἰδώς is the feeling of *innate moral repugnance* to doing a dishonorable act. This moral repugnance is not found in αἰσχύνη, which is rather the feeling of *disgrace* which results from doing an unworthy thing, or the fear of such disgrace which serves to prevent its being done. αἰδώς is thus the nobler word, αἰσχύνη having regard chiefly to the opinions of others. αἰδώς is the fear of doing a shameful thing, αἰσχύνη is chiefly the fear of being found out. "αἰδώς would always restrain a good man from an unworthy act, while αἰσχύνη might sometimes restrain a bad one" (Trench). ἐντροπή stands somewhat between the other two words in meaning, but in the N.T. leans to the nobler side, indicating that *wholesome shame* which leads a man to consideration of his condition if it is unworthy, and to a change of conduct for the better. σωφροσύνη, *self-command*, may not seem to have much in common with these three words. As a matter of fact, however, it expresses positively that which αἰδώς expresses negatively.

SYNONYM DISTINCTIONS

§ 6. Prayer.

εὐχή, προσευχή, δέησις, ἔντευξις, εὐχαριστία, αἴτημα, ἱκετηρία.

εὐχή, when it means *prayer*, has apparently a general signification. προσευχή and δέησις are often used together. προσευχή is restricted to prayer to God, while δέησις has no such restriction. δέησις also refers chiefly to prayer *for particular benefits*, while προσευχή is more general. The prominent thought in ἔντευξις is that of boldness and freedom in approach to God. εὐχαριστία is *thanksgiving*, the grateful acknowledgment of God's mercies, chiefly in prayer. αἴτημα, much like δέησις, denotes a specific petition for a particular thing. In ἱκετηρία the attitude of humility and deprecation in prayer is specially emphasized. All these words may indicate at times not different kinds of prayer, but the same prayer viewed from different stand-points.

§ 7. To rebuke; rebuke, accusation.

ἐπιτιμάω, ἐλέγχω; αἰτία, ἔλεγχος.

ἐπιτιμάω means simply *to rebuke*, in any sense. It may be justly or unjustly, and, if justly, the rebuke may be heeded or it may not. ἐλέγχω, on the other hand, means to rebuke with sufficient cause, and also effectually, so as to bring the one rebuked to a confession or at least a conviction of sin. In other words, it means *to convince*. A similar distinction exists between the nouns αἰτία and ἔλεγχος. αἰτία is an accusation, whether false or true. ἔλεγχος is a charge which is shown to be true, and often is so confessed by the accused. It has both a judicial and a moral meaning.

§ 8. Boaster, proud, insolent.

ἀλαζών, ὑπερήφανος, ὑβριστής.

ἀλαζών is properly *a boaster*, who tells great things concerning his own prowess and achievements, with the implied idea that many of his claims are false. This word naturally describes a trait which manifests itself in contact with one's fellow-men, not one which exists simply within the heart. ὑπερήφανος describes one who thinks too highly of himself, describing a trait which is simply internal, not referring primarily to external manifestation, although this is implied. It means one who is *proud*, the external manifestation when it appears being in the form of *arrogance* in dealing with others. ὑβριστής describes one who delights in *insolent wrong-doing* toward others,

SYNONYM DISTINCTIONS

finds pleasure in such acts. Cruelty and lust are two of the many forms which this quality assumes. These three words occur together in Ro. i. 30. They are never used in a good sense. They may be said to move in a certain sense in an ascending scale of guilt, designating respectively "the boastful *in words*, the proud and overbearing *in thoughts*, the insolent and injurious *in acts*" (Cremer).

§ 9. Incorruptible, unfading.

ἄφθαρτος, ἀμάραντος, ἀμαράντινος.

ἄφθαρτος is properly *incorruptible*, unaffected by corruption and decay. It is applied to God, and to that which is connected with him. ἀμάραντος expresses the same idea in another way. It means *unfading*, the root idea being that it is unaffected by the withering which is common in the case of flowers. ἀμαράντινος, derived from ἀμάραντος, means *composed of amaranths, i.e* of unfading flowers.

§ 10. Faultless, unblamed.

ἄμωμος, ἄμεμπτος, ἀνέγκλητος, ἀνεπίληπτος.

ἄμωμος is *faultless, without blemish, free from imperfections*. It refers especially to character. ἄμεμπτος is strictly *unblamed*, one with whom no fault is found. This of course refers particularly to the verdict of others upon one. ἀνέγκλητος designates one against whom there is no accusation, implying not acquittal of a charge, but that no charge has been made. ἀνεπίληπτος means *irreprehensible*, designating one who affords nothing upon which an adversary might seize, in order to make a charge against him.

§ 11. Regeneration, renovation.

παλιγγενεσία, ἀνακαίνωσις.

παλιγγενεσία means *new birth*. In classical Greek it was used in a weakened sense to denote a recovery, restoration, revival. In the N.T. it is used only twice, but in a higher sense. In Tit. iii. 5 it means *new birth, regeneration*, referring to God's act of causing the sinner to pass from the death of sin into spiritual life in Christ. It has a wider meaning in Mat. xix. 28, where it is used of the change which is ultimately to take place in all the universe, its regeneration, which is the full working out of the change involved in the regeneration of the individual. ἀνακαίνωσις is *renewal* or

SYNONYM DISTINCTIONS

renovation, denoting a continuous process through which man becomes more fully Christ-like, in which process he is a worker together with God. Some, as *e.g.* Cremer, without sufficient reason, have thought that the early use of παλιγγενεσία as a somewhat technical term, to denote the Pythagorean doctrine of transmigration, gave to the word a permanent eschatological coloring, so that in the N.T. it has the meaning *resurrection*, especially in Mat. xix. 28.

§ 12. Murderer.

φονεύς, ἀνθρωποκτόνος, σικάριος.

Both in derivation and usage, φονεύς and ἀνθρωποκτόνος are distinguished from each other just as the English *murderer* from *manslayer* or *homicide*. σικάριος, used only in Ac. xxi. 38, is the Latin *sicarius*, and means *an assassin*, usually hired for the work, who furtively stabbed his enemy with a short sword, the Latin *sica*. φονεύς is a generic word and may denote a murderer of any kind, σικάριος being one of the specific varieties which it includes.

§ 13. Anti-Christ, false Christ.

ψευδόχριστος, ἀντίχριστος.

ψευδόχριστος means *a false Christ, a pretended Messiah*, who sets himself up instead of Christ, proclaiming that he is Christ. Some have given about the same meaning to ἀντίχριστος. But it is much more probable that it means one diametrically opposed to Christ, one who sets himself up against Christ, proclaiming that there is no Christ.

§ 14. Profligacy.

ἀσωτία, ἀσέλγεια.

The fundamental idea of ἀσωτία is " wastefulness and riotous excess ; of ἀσέλγεια, lawless insolence and wanton caprice" (Trench). ἀσωτία means reckless and extravagant expenditure, chiefly for the gratification of one's sensual desires. It denotes a dissolute, profligate course of life. In ἀσέλγεια also there is included the idea of profligacy, often of lasciviousness, but the fundamental thought is the acknowledging of no restraints, the insolent doing of whatever one's caprice may suggest.

SYNONYM DISTINCTIONS

§ 15. Covenant-breaker, implacable.

ἀσύνθετος, ἄσπονδος.

These words are quite similar in their effects, but opposite in their conception. ἀσύνθετος, occurring only in Ro. i. 31, is *covenant-breaker*, one who interrupts a state of peace and brings on war by disregarding an agreement by which peace is maintained. ἄσπονδος is *implacable*, one who refuses to agree to any terms or suggestions of peace. It implies a state of war, and a refusal of covenant or even of armistice to end it permanently or temporarily. In the N.T. use both words probably refer not to war in the strict sense so much as to discord and strife.

§ 16. Beautiful, graceful.

ἀστεῖος, ὡραῖος, καλός.

ἀστεῖος is properly one living in a city, urban. It soon acquires the meaning *urbane, polite, elegant*. Then it obtains to a limited extent the meaning *beautiful*, although never in the highest degree. ὡραῖος, from ὥρα, hour, period, means properly *timely*. From that comes the idea of being beautiful, since nearly everything is beautiful in its hour of fullest perfection. καλός is a much higher word. It means *beautiful*, physically or morally. It is, however, distinctly the beauty which comes from harmony, the beauty which arises from a symmetrical adjustment in right proportion, in other words, from the harmonious completeness of the object concerned.

§ 17. Wisdom, knowledge.

σοφία, φρόνησις, γνῶσις, ἐπίγνωσις.

σοφία is certainly the highest word of all these. It is properly *wisdom*. It denotes mental excellence in the highest and fullest sense, expressing an *attitude* as well as an *act* of the mind. It comprehends knowledge and implies goodness, including the striving after the highest ends, as well as the using of the best means for their attainment. It is never ascribed to any one but God and good men, except in a plainly ironical sense. φρόνησις is a middle term, sometimes having a meaning nearly as high as σοφία, sometimes much lower. It means *prudence, intelligence*, a skillful adaptation of the means to the end desired, the end, however, not being necessarily a good one. γνῶσις is *knowledge, cognition*, the understanding of facts or truths,

SYNONYM DISTINCTIONS

or else *insight, discernment*. ἐπίγνωσις has an intensive meaning as compared with γνῶσις, it is a fuller, clearer, more thorough knowledge. The verb ἐπιγινώσκω has the same intensive force as compared with γινώσκω.

§ 18. Religious.

θεοσεβής, εὐσεβής, εὐλαβής, θρῆσκος, δεισιδαίμων.

θεοσεβής, according to derivation and usage, means *worship of God* (or of the gods), a fulfillment of one's duty towards God. It is a general term, meaning *religious* in a good sense. **εὐσεβής** is distinguished from θεοσεβής in two ways. It is used to include the fulfillment of obligations of all kinds, both towards God and man. It is thus applied to the fulfillment of the duties involved in human relations, as towards one's parents. Furthermore, when used in the higher sense, it means not any kind of worship, but, as the etymology indicates, the worshipping of God *aright*. **εὐλαβής**, meaning originally *careful in handling*, in its religious application means careful in handling divine things. It characterizes the anxious and scrupulous worshipper, careful not to change anything that should be observed in worship, and fearful of offending. It means *devout*, and may be applied to an adherent of any religion, being especially appropriate to describe the best of the Jewish worshippers. **θρῆσκος** is one who is diligent in the performance of the *outward* service of God. It applies especially to ceremonial worship. **δεισιδαίμων**, in accordance with its derivation, makes prominent the element of *fear*. It emphasizes strongly the ideas of dependence and of anxiety for divine favor. It may be used as practically equivalent to θεοσεβής. Often, however, it implies that the fear which it makes prominent is an unworthy fear, so that it comes to have the meaning *superstitious*. In the N.T. it is used, as is also the noun δεισιδαιμονία, in a purposely neutral sense, meaning simply *religious*, neither conveying the highest meaning, nor plainly implying a lower meaning.

§ 19. Pure.

εἰλικρινής, καθαρός, ἀμίαντος.

εἰλικρινής denotes chiefly that which is pure as being *sincere*, free from foreign admixture. **καθαρός** is that which is pure as being *clean*, free from soil or stain. The meaning of both in the N.T. is distinctly ethical. **ἀμίαντος** is *unspotted*, describing that which is far removed from every kind of contamination.

SYNONYM DISTINCTIONS

§ 20. Assembly, church.

συναγωγή, ἐκκλησία, πανήγυρις.

According to their derivation, **συναγωγή** is simply *an assembly*, a mass of people gathered together; **ἐκκλησία** is a narrower word, also *an assembly*, but including only those specially *called together out of* a larger multitude, for the transaction of business. ἐκκλησία usually denotes a somewhat more select company than συναγωγή. A significant use of ἐκκλησία in strict harmony with its derivation was common among the Greeks. It was their common word for the lawful assembly in a free Greek city of all those possessing the rights of citizenship, for the transaction of public affairs. They were *summoned out of* the whole population, "a select portion of it, including neither the populace, nor strangers, nor yet those who had forfeited their civic rights" (Trench). συναγωγή had been, before N.T. times, appropriated to designate *a synagogue*, a Jewish assembly for worship, distinct from the Temple, in which sense it is used in the N.T. Probably for that reason, and also for its greater inherent etymological fitness, ἐκκλησία is the word taken to designate *a Christian church*, a company of believers who meet for worship. Both these words, however, are sometimes used in the N.T. in a non-technical sense. **πανήγυρις**, occurring only in Heb. xii. 23, differs from both, denoting a solemn assembly for festal rejoicing.

§ 21. Humility, gentleness.

ταπεινοφροσύνη, πραότης.

ταπεινοφροσύνη is *humility*, not the making of one's self small when he is really great, but thinking little of one's self, because this is in a sense the right estimate for any human being, however great. **πραότης** is founded upon this idea, and goes beyond it. It is the attitude of mind and behavior which, arising from humility, disposes one to receive with *gentleness* and *meekness* whatever may come to him from others or from God.

§ 22. Gentleness.

πραότης, ἐπιείκεια.

Both words may be translated *gentleness*, yet there are marked differences in meaning. **πραότης** is rather passive, denoting, as has been said above, see § 21, one's attitude toward others in view of their acts, bad or

21

SYNONYM DISTINCTIONS

good. ἐπιείκεια is distinctly active, it is seen in one's deeds toward others, and it usually implies the relation of superior to inferior. It is fundamentally a relaxing of strict legal requirements concerning others, yet doing this in order more fully to carry out the real spirit of the law. It is *clemency* in which there is no element of weakness or injustice.

§ 23. Desire, lust.

ἐπιθυμία, πάθος, ὁρμή, ὄρεξις.

ἐπιθυμία is the broadest of these words. Its meaning may be good, but it is usually bad. It denotes any natural desire or appetite, usually with the implication that it is a depraved desire. πάθος has not as broad a meaning as in classical Greek, but denotes evil desire, chiefly, however, as a condition of the soul rather than in active operation. ὁρμή indicates *hostile* motion toward an object, either for seizing or repelling. ὄρεξις is a desire or appetite, especially seeking the object of gratification in order to make it one's own.

§ 24. Affliction.

θλῖψις, στενοχωρία.

θλῖψις according to its derivation means *pressure*. In its figurative sense it is that which presses upon the spirit, *affliction*. στενοχωρία meant originally *a narrow, confined space*. It denotes affliction as arising from cramping circumstances. In use it cannot always be distinguished from θλῖψις, but it is ordinarily a stronger word.

§ 25. Bad, evil.

κακός, πονηρός, φαῦλος.

These words may be used with very little distinction of meaning, but often the difference is marked. κακός frequently means *evil* rather negatively, referring to the absence of the qualities which constitute a person or thing what it should be or what it claims to be. It is also used meaning *evil* in a moral sense. It is a general antithesis to ἀγαθός. πονηρός is a word at once stronger and more active, it means *mischief-making*, delighting in injury, doing evil to others, dangerous, destructive. κακός describes the quality according to its nature, πονηρός, according to its effects. φαῦλος is the bad chiefly as the *worthless*, the good for nothing.

SYNONYM DISTINCTIONS

§ 26. Punishment.

τιμωρία, κόλασις.

τιμωρία in classical and N.T. usage denotes especially the vindicative character of punishment, it is the punishment in relation to the *punisher*. κόλασις in classical Greek meant usually punishment which aimed at the reformation of the offender. But sometimes in later Greek, and always in the N.T., the idea of reformation seems to disappear, so that there remains simply the idea of punishment, but viewed in relation to the *punished*.

§ 27. To pollute.

μιαίνω, μολύνω.

μιαίνω meant originally *to stain*, as with color. μολύνω meant originally *to smear over*, as with mud or filth, always having a bad meaning, while the meaning of μιαίνω might be either good or bad. According to classical Greek, μιαίνω has a religious meaning, *to profane*, while μολύνω is simply *to spoil, disgrace*. As ethically applied in the N.T. they have both practically the same meaning, *to pollute, defile*. It is, however, true that μιαίνω, to judge from classical usage, refers chiefly to the effect of the act not on the individual, but on others, on the community.

§ 28. To do.

ποιέω, πράσσω.

These words are often used interchangeably, but in many cases a distinction can be drawn. ποιέω refers more to the object and end of an act, πράσσω rather to the means by which the object is attained. Hence, while ποιέω means *to accomplish*, πράσσω may mean nothing more than merely *to busy one's self about*. ποιέω often means to do a thing once for all, πράσσω, to do continually or repeatedly. From these distinctions it follows that ποιέω, being on the whole the higher word, is more often used of doing good, πράσσω more frequently of doing evil.

§ 29. Fleshly, fleshy, sensual.

σαρκικός, σάρκινος, ψυχικός.

σαρκικός means *fleshly*, that which is controlled by the wrong desires which rule in the flesh, flesh often being understood in its broad sense, see

SYNONYM DISTINCTIONS

σάρξ. It describes a man who gives the flesh the dominion in his life, a place which does not belong to it by right. It means distinctly opposed to the Spirit of God, anti-spiritual. σάρκινος properly means *fleshy*, made of flesh, flesh being the material of which it is composed. When given a bad meaning, however, it is plainly similar to σαρκικός, but according to Trench not so strong, denoting one as unspiritual, undeveloped, rather than anti-spiritual. Others, as Cremer and Thayer, with more probability make σάρκινος the stronger, it describes one who is flesh, wholly given up to the flesh, rooted in the flesh, rather than one who simply acts according to the flesh (σαρκικός). There is much confusion between the two in the N.T. manuscripts. ψυχικός has a meaning somewhat similar to σαρκικός. Both are used in contrast with πνευματικός. But ψυχικός has really a distinct meaning, describing the life which is controlled by the ψυχή. It denotes, therefore, that which belongs to the animal life, or that which is controlled simply by the appetites and passions of the sensuous nature.

§ 30. Mercy, compassion.

ἔλεος, οἰκτιρμός.

Both words denote sympathy, fellow-feeling with misery, mercy, compassion. ἔλεος, however, manifests itself chiefly in acts rather than words, while οἰκτιρμός is used rather of the inward feeling of compassion which abides in the heart. A criminal might ask for ἔλεος, *mercy*, from his judge; but hopeless suffering may be the object of οἰκτιρμός, *compassion*.

§ 31. To love.

ἀγαπάω, φιλέω.

ἀγαπάω, and not φιλέω, is the word used of God's love to men, φιλανθρωπία is, however, once used with this meaning, Tit. iii. 4. ἀγαπάω is also the word ordinarily used of men's love to God, but φιλέω is once so used, 1 Cor. xvi. 22. ἀγαπάω is the word used of love to one's enemies. The interchange of the words in Jn. xxi. 15–17 is very interesting and instructive.

§ 32. To will, to wish.

βούλομαι, θέλω.

In many cases these two words are used without appreciable distinction, meaning *conscious willing, purpose*. But frequently it is evident that a

SYNONYM DISTINCTIONS

difference is intended, although there is much difference of opinion as to the exact distinction. Thayer says that βούλομαι "seems to designate the will which follows deliberation," θέλω, "the will which proceeds from inclination." Grimm, on the other hand, says that θέλω gives prominence to the emotive element, βούλομαι to the rational and volitive; θέλω signifies the choice, while βούλομαι marks the choice as deliberate and intelligent. The view of Cremer on the whole seems preferable to any other. According to this view, βούλομαι has the wider range of meaning, but θέλω is the stronger word, θέλω denotes the active resolution, the will urging on to action, see Ro. vii. 15, while βούλομαι is rather to have in thought, to intend, to be determined. βούλομαι sometimes means no more than to have an inclination, see Ac. xxiii. 15. Instructive examples of the use of the two words in close proximity are found in Mar. xv. 9, 15, and especially Mat. i. 19.

§ 33. Schism.

σχίσμα, αἵρεσις.

σχίσμα is *actual division, separation.* αἵρεσις is rather *the separating tendency,* so it is really more fundamental than σχίσμα.

§ 34. Mind, understanding.

νοῦς, διάνοια.

νοῦς is distinctly *the reflective consciousness,* "the organ of moral thinking and knowing, the intellectual organ of moral sentiment" (Cremer). διάνοια meant originally *activity of thinking,* but has borrowed from νοῦς its common meaning of *faculty of thought.* It is more common than νοῦς, and has largely replaced it in its usual meanings.

§ 35. Law.

νόμος, θεσμός, ἐντολή, δόγμα.

νόμος is the common word meaning *law.* It may mean law in general. In the N.T., however, it usually means the law of God, and most frequently the Mosaic law. θεσμός is law considered with special reference to the authority on which it rests. ἐντολή is more specific, being used of a particular command. δόγμα is an authoritative conclusion, a proposition which it is expected that all will recognize as universally binding.

SYNONYM DISTINCTIONS

§ 36. Type, image.
τύπος, ἀντίτυπος.

τύπος has many meanings, among the most common being *image, pattern* or *model*, and *type*. In the last sense it means a person or thing prefiguring a future person or thing, *e.g.*, Adam as a type of Christ, Ro. v. 14. ἀντίτυπος, as used in 1 Pet. iii. 21, is by Thayer and many others thought to correspond to τύπος as its counterpart, in the sense which the English word antitype suggests. By Cremer it is rather given the meaning *image*.

§ 37. To ask.
αἰτέω, ἐρωτάω.

Thayer, as opposed to Trench and others, would make the distinction between these two words to be this: "αἰτέω signifies to ask for something to be given, not done, giving prominence to the thing asked for rather than the person, and hence is rarely used in exhortation. ἐρωτάω, on the other hand, is to request a person to do (rarely to give) something; referring more directly to the person, it is naturally used in exhortation, etc."

§ 38. World, age.
αἰών, κόσμος.

It is only in a part of their meanings that these two words are in any real sense synonymous, and it is that part which is here considered. Both A. V. and R. V. often translate αἰών by *world*, thus obscuring the distinction between it and κόσμος. αἰών is usually better expressed by *age*, it is the world at a given time, a particular period in the world's history. κόσμος has very frequently an unfavorable meaning, denoting the inhabitants of the world, mankind in general, as opposed to God. A similar meaning is often attached to αἰών, it means the spirit of the age, often in an unfavorable sense. See Ep. ii. 2, where both words occur together. An exceptional meaning for the plural of αἰών is found in Heb. i. 2 and xi. 3, where it denotes the worlds, apparently in reference to space rather than time.

§ 39. Rest.
ἀνάπαυσις, ἄνεσις.

Both words in a certain sense mean *rest*, but from different standpoints. ἀνάπαυσις is rest which comes by cessation from labor, which may

SYNONYM DISTINCTIONS

be simply temporary. ἄνεσις means literally the relaxation of strings which have been drawn tight. Hence, it is used to designate ease, especially that which comes by relaxation of unfavorable conditions of any kind, such as affliction.

§ 40. Wind.

πνεῦμα, πνοή, ἄνεμος, λαῖλαψ, θύελλα.

πνεῦμα when used in its lower meaning to denote wind means simply *an ordinary wind*, a regularly blowing current of air of considerable force. πνοή is distinguished from it as being a gentler motion of the air. ἄνεμος, on the other hand, is more forcible than πνεῦμα, it is the strong, often the tempestuous, wind. λαῖλαψ is the violent fitful wind which accompanies a heavy shower. θύελλα is more violent than any of the others, and often implies a conflict of opposing winds.

§ 41. Old.

παλαιός, ἀρχαῖος.

According to their derivation, παλαιός is that which has been in existence for a long time, ἀρχαῖος that which has been from the beginning. In use, at times no distinction can be drawn. Often, however, ἀρχαῖος does denote distinctively that which has been from the beginning, and so it reaches back to a point of time beyond παλαιός. παλαιός has often the secondary meaning of that which is old and so worn out, having suffered more or less from the injuries and ravages of time, its opposite in this sense being καινός.

§ 42. Harsh, austere.

αὐστηρός, σκληρός.

αὐστηρός has not necessarily an unfavorable meaning. It is well represented by the word *austere*, it means one who is earnest and severe, strict in his ways, opposed to all levity. By implication it may have the unfavorable meaning of harshness or moroseness. σκληρός has always an unfavorable meaning. It indicates one who is uncivil, intractable, rough and harsh. There is in it the implication of inhumanity.

SYNONYM DISTINCTIONS

§ 43. Darkness.

σκότος, γνόφος, ζόφος, ἀχλύς.

σκότος is a general word, meaning *darkness* in any sense. **γνόφος** usually refers to darkness that accompanies a storm. **ζόφος** meant originally *the gloom* of twilight. It was then applied in classical Greek to the darkness of the underworld, the gloom of a sunless region. The latter meaning seems to be practically the one which the word has in the N.T. **ἀχλύς** is specifically a misty darkness.

§ 44. People, nation.

λαός, ἔθνος, δῆμος, ὄχλος.

λαός is a word which is usually limited in use to the chosen people, Israel. **ἔθνος** in the singular is a general term for nation, applied to any nation, even to the Jews. In the plural it ordinarily denotes all mankind aside from the Jews and in contrast with them, the Gentiles. **δῆμος** is a people, especially organized and convened together, and exercising their rights as citizens. **ὄχλος** is *a crowd*, an unorganized multitude, especially composed of those who have not the rights and privileges of free citizens.

§ 45. Servant, slave.

δοῦλος, θεράπων, διάκονος, οἰκέτης, ὑπηρέτης.

δοῦλος is the usual word for *slave*, one who is permanently in servitude, in subjection to a master. **θεράπων** is simply one who renders service at a particular time, sometimes as a slave, more often as a freeman, who renders voluntary service prompted by duty or love. It denotes one who serves, *in his relation to a person*. **διάκονος** also may designate either a slave or a freeman, it denotes a servant viewed *in relation to his work*. **οἰκέτης** designates a slave, sometimes being practically equivalent to δοῦλος. Usually, however, as the etymology of the term indicates, it means a slave as a member of the household, not emphasizing the servile idea, but rather the relation which would tend to mitigate the severity of his condition. **ὑπηρέτης** means literally *an under-rower*, and was used to describe an ordinary rower on a war-galley. It is then used, as in the N.T., to indicate any man, not a slave, who served in a subordinate position under a superior.

SYNONYM DISTINCTIONS

§ 46. To adulterate.

καπηλεύω, δολόω.

Both these words mean *to adulterate*, and some maintain that they are practically identical. But it is more probable that **δολόω** means simply to adulterate, while **καπηλεύω** conveys the idea of adulterating for the sake of making an unjust profit by the process.

§ 47. Animal.

ζῶον, θηρίον.

ζῶον is a general term, meaning *living creature*, which may include all living beings, in classical Greek even including man. In the N.T. it means ordinarily *animal*. **θηρίον** is *beast*, usually wild beast. It implies perhaps not necessarily wildness and ferocity, but at least a certain amount of brutality which is wanting in ζῶον. ζῶον emphasizes the qualities in which animals are akin to man, θηρίον, those in which they are inferior.

§ 48. Sea.

θάλασσα, πέλαγος.

θάλασσα is the more general word, indicating *the sea* or *ocean* as contrasted with the land or shore. It may be applied to small bodies of water. **πέλαγος** is *the open sea*, the uninterrupted expanse of water, in contrast with the portions broken by islands or with partly inclosed bays. The prominent thought is said by Trench to be breadth rather than depth. Noteworthy is the distinction between the two words in Mat. xviii. 6.

§ 49. To grieve.

λυπέομαι, πενθέω, θρηνέω, κόπτομαι.

λυπέομαι is the most general word, meaning simply *to grieve*, outwardly or inwardly. **πενθέω** means properly *to lament for the dead*. It is also applied to passionate lamentation of any kind, so great that it cannot be hid. **θρηνέω** is *to give utterance to a dirge* over the dead, either in unstudied words, or in a more elaborate poem. This word is used by S. in describing David's lament over Saul and Jonathan. **κόπτομαι** is *to beat the breast in grief*, ordinarily for the dead.

SYNONYM DISTINCTIONS

§ 50. Form, appearance.

ἰδέα, μορφή, σχῆμα.

ἰδέα denotes merely *outward appearance*. Both **μορφή** and **σχῆμα** express something more than that. They too denote outward form, but as including one's habits, activities and modes of action in general. In μορφή it is also implied that the outward form expresses the inner essence, an idea which is absent from σχῆμα. μορφή expresses the form as that which is intrinsic and essential, σχῆμα signifies the figure, shape, as that which is more outward and accidental. Both σχῆμα and ἰδέα therefore deal with externals, σχῆμα being more comprehensive than ἰδέα, while μορφή deals with externals as expressing that which is internal.

§ 51. Clothing.

ἱμάτιον, χιτών, ἱματισμός, χλαμύς, στολή, ποδήρης.

ἱμάτιον is used in a general sense to mean *clothing*, and may thus be applied to any garment when it is not desired to express its exact nature. In a more specific use, however, it denotes the large loose outer garment, *a cloak*, which ordinarily was worn, but in working was laid aside. **χιτών** is best expressed by the word *tunic*. It was a closely fitting under-garment, usually worn next the skin. At times, especially in working, it was the only garment worn. A person clothed only in the χιτών was often called γυμνός (Jn. xxi. 7). ἱμάτιον and χιτών are often found associated as the upper and under garment respectively. **ἱματισμός** does not denote a specific garment, but means *clothing*, being used, however, ordinarily only of garments more or less stately or costly. **χλαμύς** is *a robe* or *cloak*, it is a technical expression for a garment of dignity or office. **στολή** is any stately robe, ordinarily long, reaching to the feet or sweeping the ground, often worn by women. **ποδήρης** was originally an adjective meaning *reaching to the feet*. It can hardly be distinguished in use from στολή. It occurs only in Rev. i. 13.

§ 52. New.

νέος, καινός.

νέος is *the new* as contemplated under the aspect of time, that which has recently come into existence. **καινός** is *the new* under the aspect of quality, that which has not seen service. καινός therefore often means new

SYNONYM DISTINCTIONS

as contrasted with that which has decayed with age, or is worn out, its opposite then being παλαιός. It sometimes suggests that which is unusual. It often implies praise, the new as superior to the old. Occasionally, on the other hand, it implies the opposite, the new as inferior to that which is old, because the old is familiar or because it has improved with age. Of course it is evident that both νέος and καινός may sometimes be applied to the same object, but from different points of view.

§ 53. Labor.

μόχθος, πόνος, κόπος.

μόχθος is *labor*, hard and often painful. It is the ordinary word for common labor which is the usual lot of humanity. **πόνος** is *labor* which demands one's whole strength. It is therefore applied to labors of an unusual kind, specially wearing or painful. In classical Greek it was the usual word employed to describe the labors of Hercules. **κόπος** denotes *the weariness* which results from labor, or labor considered from the stand-point of the resulting weariness.

§ 54. Drunkenness, drinking.

μέθη, πότος, οἰνοφλυγία, κῶμος, κραιπάλη.

μέθη is the ordinary word for *drunkenness*. **πότος** is rather concrete, *a drinking, carousing*. **οἰνοφλυγία** is a prolonged condition of drunkenness, *a debauch*. **κῶμος** includes *riot* and *revelry*, usually as arising from drunkenness. **κραιπάλη** denotes *the sickness* and *discomfort* resulting from drunkenness.

§ 55. War, battle.

πόλεμος, μάχη.

πόλεμος ordinarily means *war*, i.e., the whole course of hostilities; **μάχη**, *battle*, a single engagement. It is also true that μάχη has often the weaker force of *strife* or *contention*, which is very seldom found in πόλεμος.

§ 56. Basket.

σπυρίς, κόφινος.

These words in the N.T. are used with an evident purpose to discriminate between them. The distinction, however, does not seem to have

SYNONYM DISTINCTIONS

been chiefly one of size, as some have thought, but of use. σπυρίς is usually a basket for food, *a lunch-basket, a hamper*, while κόφινος is a more general term for *basket*. The descriptions of the two miracles of feeding the multitude use always different words in the two cases, see *e.g.* Mar. viii. 19, 20.

§ 57. It is necessary.

δεῖ, ὀφείλει.

δεῖ, the third person of δέω, is commonly used impersonally in classical Greek. This usage is less common, but frequent, in the N.T. δεῖ indicates a necessity in the nature of things rather than a personal obligation, it describes that which *must* be done. ὀφείλει indicates rather the personal obligation, it is that which is proper, something that *ought* to be done.

§ 58. Tax.

φόρος, τέλος, κῆνσος, δίδραχμον.

φόρος indicates *a direct tax* which was levied annually on houses, lands, and persons, and paid usually in produce. τέλος is *an indirect tax* on merchandise, which was collected at piers, harbors, and gates of cities. It was similar to modern import duties. κῆνσος, originally an enrollment of property and persons, came to mean *a poll-tax*, levied annually on individuals by the Roman government. δίδραχμον was the coin used to pay an annual tax levied by the religious leaders of Israel for the purpose of defraying the general expenses of the Temple.

§ 59. Tax-collector.

τελώνης, ἀρχιτελώνης.

The Roman system of collecting taxes, especially the τέλοι, in their provinces, included ordinarily three grades of officials. There was the highest, called in Latin *publicanus*, who paid a sum of money for the taxes of a certain province, and then exacted that and as much more as he could from the province. This man lived in Rome. Then there were the *submagistri*, who had charge each of a certain portion of territory, and who lived in the provinces. Then there were the *portitores*, the actual customhouse officers, who did the real work of collecting the taxes. The N.T. word τελώνης is used to describe one of the *portitores*, it is the lowest of these three grades. It does not correspond to the Latin *publicanus*, and the word *publican* used to translate it in A. V. and R. V. is apt to be misleading, *tax-collector* would be better. ἀρχιτελώνης, only occurring in Lu. xix. 2, evidently describes a higher official than τελώνης, and is probably one of the *submagistri*, the next higher grade.

§ 60. Child.

τέκνον, υἱός, παῖς, παιδίον, παιδάριον, παιδίσκη.

τέκνον and **υἱός** both point to parentage. τέκνον, however, emphasizes the idea of descent, giving prominence to the physical and outward aspects; while υἱός emphasizes the idea of relationship, and considers especially the inward, ethical, and legal aspects. **παῖς** as well as τέκνον emphasizes the idea of descent, but gives especial prominence to age, denoting a child as one who is young. παῖς is also often used of a servant. The number of years covered by the term παῖς is quite indefinite. Its diminutives **παιδίον** and **παιδάριον** are used without appreciable difference to denote a young child. (παιδίσκος in classical Greek and) **παιδίσκη**, in which the diminutive force is largely lost, cover the years of late childhood and early youth.

§ 61. Tribe, family, household.

φυλή, πατριά, οἶκος.

These words form a series. **φυλή** is sometimes *a race, nation*, but usually *a tribe*, such as one of the twelve tribes of Israel, descended from the twelve sons of Jacob. **πατριά** is a smaller division within the tribe, it is an association of families closely related, in the N.T. generally used of those descended from a particular one of the sons of Jacob's sons. **οἶκος** is yet narrower, *household*, including all the inmates of a single house, being the unit of organization.

SYNONYM DISTINCTIONS

Abbreviations for Pages 35-39

acc.	accusative
BU.	Alexander Buttman's *Grammar of New Testament Greek*
Gr.	S. G. Green's *Handbook to the Grammar of the Greek New Testament*
i.e.	that is
S.	Septuagint
W.H.	Westcott and Hort's *The New Testament in the Original Greek*
Wi.	G. B. Winer's *Grammar of the Idiom of the New Testament*
*	indicates that all the passages in which a word occurs in the New Testament have been given

SYNONYM DISTINCTIONS

ἀγαθωσύνη, ης, ἡ, *goodness*, 2 Th. i. 11. (S.) *Syn.:* ἀγαθωσύνη emphasizes the *zeal for goodness;* χρηστότης, *kindness, benignity.*

ἀγαπάω, ῶ, ήσω, *to love*, Lu. vii. 47; *to wish well to*, Mat. v. 43, xix. 19; *to take pleasure in*, Heb. i. 9; *to long for*, 2 Tim. iv. 8. *Syn.:* ἀγαπάω denotes the love of the reason, esteem; φιλέω, the love of the feelings, warm instinctive affection.

ἀ-γράμματος, ον, *unlearned*, *i.e.*, in Rabbinical lore, Ac. iv. 13.* *Syn.:* ἀγράμματος means *illiterate*, without knowledge gained by study; ἰδιώτης, not a specialist, or without knowledge gained by mingling in public life.

αἰτέω, ῶ, ήσω, *to ask, pray, require*, Ja. i. 6; usually with two accs., or acc. of thing and ἀπό or παρά (gen.) of person; mid., *to ask for one's self, beg*, Jn. xvi. 26. *Syn.:* αἰτέω is to ask a favor, as a suppliant; ἐρωτάω, to ask a question, or as an equal; πυνθάνομαι, to ask for information.

αἰών, ῶνος, ὁ (ἀεί), originally *an indefinitely long period of time, an age;* hence, (1) *an unbroken age, eternity*, past, as Ac. xv. 18; future, 2 Pet. iii. 18, especially in the following phrases: εἰς τὸν αἰῶνα, *for ever*, with negative adv. *never;* εἰς τοὺς αἰῶνας, a stronger expression, *for evermore;* εἰς τοὺς αἰῶνας τῶν αἰώνων, stronger still (see Gr. § 327, ii, Wi. § 36, 2), *for ever and ever.* Phrase slightly varied, Ep. iii. 21; Heb. i. 8; 2 Pet. iii. 18; Ju. 25; Rev. xiv. 11; (2) in plur., *the worlds, the universe*, Heb. i. 2, xi. 3; (3) *the present age* (ὁ αἰὼν οὗτος, ὁ ἐνεστὼς αἰών, ὁ νῦν αἰών), Gal. i. 4; 1 Tim. vi. 17, in contrast with the time after the second coming of Christ, *the coming age* (ὁ αἰὼν ἐκεῖνος, αἰὼν μέλλων, ὁ αἰὼν ὁ ἐρχόμενος, οἱ αἰῶνες οἱ ἐπερχόμενοι), Lu. xx. 35, xviii. 30; Ep. ii. 7; Mat. xii. 32. *Syn.:* αἰών is the world under the aspect of *time;* κόσμος, under that of *space.*

ἀλείφω, ψω, *to anoint*, festally, or in homage, also medicinally, or in embalming the dead, Mar. xvi. 1, Lu. vii. 46. *Syn.:* χρίω has always a religious and symbolical force, which is absent in ἀλείφω.

ἀληθής, ές (ἀ, λαθ- in λανθάνω), *unconcealed, true*, Ac. xii. 9; Jn. iv. 18; *truthful*, Mat. xxii. 16; Mar. xii. 14. *Syn.:* ἀληθής means true *morally*, faithful; ἀληθινός, *genuine*, in contrast either with the *false* or the *imperfect*.

ἄλλος, η, ο, *other, another*, Mar. vi. 15; ὁ ἄλλος, *the other*, Mat. v. 39; οἱ ἄλλοι, *the others, the rest. Syn.:* ἄλλος indicates that which is simply *numerically* distinct; ἕτερος, that which is generically distinct, *different*.

ἀμφί-βληστρον, ου, τό, *a fishing net*, Mat. iv. 18; Mar. i. 16 (not W. H.).* *Syn.:* σαγήνη is the *drag-net*, much larger than ἀμφίβληστρον, the *casting net;* δίκτυον is general, a net of any kind.

ἀνά-θεμα, ατος, τό, *a person* or *thing accursed*, Gal. i. 8; 1 Cor. xvi. 22; *an execration*

35

SYNONYM DISTINCTIONS

or *curse*, Ac. xxiii. 14. *Syn.*. ἀνάθημα is a thing *devoted in honor of God, consecrated*; ἀνάθεμα, simply a later form of ἀνάθημα, has come to mean *a thing devoted to destruction*.

ἀνοχή, ῆς, ἡ, *forbearance, toleration*, Ro. ii. 4, iii. 25.* *Syn.:* ὑπομονή is patience under trials, referring to *things*; μακροθυμία, patience under provocation, referring to *persons*; ἀνοχή is a forbearance *temporary* in its nature.

ἅπτω, ψω, *to kindle*, as light or fire, Lu. viii. 16, xi. 33; mid., *to touch*, Mat viii. 3; 1 Cor. vii. 1. *Syn.:* ἅπτομαι is to touch or handle; θιγγάνω, a lighter touch; ψηλαφάω, to feel or feel after.

ἄρτιος, ον, adj., *perfect, complete*, wanting in nothing, 2 Tim. iii. 17.* *Syn.:* ἄρτιος means fully adapted for its purpose; ὁλόκληρος, entire, having lost nothing; τέλειος, fully developed, complete.

ἄφ-εσις, εως, ἡ (ἀφίημι), *deliverance*; lit., only Lu. iv. 18; elsewhere always of *deliverance* from sin, remission, forgiveness, Mat. xxvi. 28; Lu. i. 77; Ep. i. 7. *Syn.:* πάρεσις is a simple *suspension of punishment* for sin, in contrast with ἄφεσις, *complete forgiveness*.

βίος, ου, ὁ, (1) *life*, as Lu. viii. 14; (2) *means of life, livelihood*, as Lu. viii. 43; (3) *goods* or *property*, as Lu. xv. 12; 1 Jn. iii. 17. *Syn.:* ζωή is life in its *principle*, and used for spiritual and immortal life; βίος is life in its *manifestations*, denoting the manner of life.

βόσκω, ήσω, *to feed*, as Mat. viii. 33; Jn. xxi. 15, 17; mid., *to feed, graze*, as Mar. v. 11. *Syn.:* ποιμαίνω is the broader word, to act as shepherd, literally or spiritually; βόσκω, simply to *feed* the flock.

βωμός, οῦ, ὁ, *an altar*, Ac. xvii. 23.* *Syn.:* βωμός is a heathen altar; θυσιαστήριον, the altar of the true God.

δειλία, ας, ἡ, *timidity, cowardice*, 2 Tim. i. 7.* *Syn.:* δειλία is always used in a bad sense; εὐλάβεια, regularly in a good sense, *pious* fear; φόβος is general, denoting either bad or good.

δεσπότης, ου, ὁ, *a lord* or *prince, a master*, as 1 Tim. vi. 1; applied to God, Lu. ii. 29; Ac. iv. 24; Ju. 4; to Christ, 2 Pet. ii. 1; Rev. vi. 10. *Syn.:* δεσπότης indicates more absolute and unlimited authority than κύριος.

δημι-ουργός, οῦ, ὁ ("a public worker"), *an artisan, a builder*, Heb. xi. 10.* *Syn.:* δημιουργός emphasizes more the idea of *power*; τεχνίτης, that of *wisdom*.

διά-δημα, ατος, τό (δέω), *a diadem, crown*, Rev. xii. 3, xiii. 1, xix. 12.* *Syn.:* διάδημα always indicates the fillet, the symbol of royalty; στέφανος is the festal *garland* of victory.

δοκέω, ῶ, δόξω, (1) *to think*, acc. and inf., Lu. viii. 18; 2 Cor. xi. 16; (2) *to seem, appear*, Lu. x. 36; Ac. xvii. 18; (3) δοκεῖ, impers., *it seems*, Mat. xvii. 25; *it seems good to* or *pleases*, dat., Lu. i. 3; Ac.

SYNONYM DISTINCTIONS

xv. 22. *Syn.*: φαίνομαι means to appear *on the outside*; δοκέω, to appear *to an individual* to be true.

δοκιμάζω, σω, *to try, scrutinize, prove*, as 2 Cor. viii. 22; Lu. xii. 56; *to judge fit, approve*, as 1 Cor. xvi. 3. *Syn.*: δοκιμάζω means to test anything with the expectation of finding it good; πειράζω, either with no expectation, or of finding it bad.

δύναμις, εως, ἡ, (1) *power, might*, absolutely or as an attribute, Lu. i. 17; Ac. iii. 12; (2) *power* over, expressed by εἰς or ἐπί (acc.), *ability to do;* (3) *exercise of power, mighty work, miracle*, as Mat. xi. 20; (4) *forces*, as of an army, spoken of the heavenly hosts, as Mat. xxiv. 29; (5) *force*, as of a word, *i.e., significance*, 1 Cor. xiv. 11. *Syn.*: τέρας indicates a miracle as a wonderful portent or prodigy; σημεῖον, as a sign, authenticating the divine mission of the doer; δύναμις, as an exhibition of divine power.

Ἑβραῖος (W. H. 'Ε-), αία, αῖον (from Heb.), also subst., ὁ, ἡ, *a Hebrew;* designating (1) any Jew, 2 Cor. xi. 22; Phil. iii. 5; (2) a Jew of Palestine, in distinction from οἱ Ἑλληνισταί, or Jews born out of Palestine, and using the Greek language, Ac. vi. 1; (3) any Jewish Christian, Heb. (heading). (S.)* *Syn.*: Ἑβραῖος denotes a Jew who spoke Aramaic or Hebrew, in distinction from Ἑλληνιστής, a Greek-speaking Jew; Ἰουδαῖος, a Jew in distinction from other nations; Ἰσραηλίτης, one of the chosen people.

ἑλκύω, σω, *to drag*, Ac. xvi. 19; *to draw*, a net, Jn. xxi. 6, 11; a sword, Jn. xviii. 10; *to draw over, to persuade*, Jn. vi. 44, xii. 32.* *Syn.*: σύρω always means to drag *by force;* ἑλκύω only *sometimes* involves force, often not.

θειότης, τητος, ἡ, *deity, divine nature*, Ro. i. 20.* *Syn.*: θειότης is deity, *abstractly;* θεότης, *personally*.

θυμός, οῦ, ὁ, *passion, great anger, wrath*, Lu. iv 28; Rev. xiv.19. *Syn.*: θυμός is *impulsive, turbulent* anger; ὀργή is anger as a *settled habit*, both may be right or wrong; παροργισμός is the bitterness of anger, always wrong.

ἱερόν, οῦ, τό (prop. neut. of ἱερός), *a temple*, used of a heathen temple, as Ac. xix. 27; of the temple at Jerusalem, as Mat. xxiv. 1; and of parts of the temple, as Mat. xii. 5. *Syn.*: ἱερόν is the whole sacred enclosure; ναός, the *shrine* itself, the holy place and the holy of holies.

καιρός, οῦ, ὁ, *a fixed time, season, opportunity*, Lu. viii. 13; Heb. xi. 15; Ac. xiv. 17; Ro. viii. 18. *Syn.*: χρόνος is time in general, viewed simply as such; καιρός, definite, suitable time, the time of some decisive event, *crisis, opportunity*.

SYNONYM DISTINCTIONS

κενός, ή, όν, *empty, vain*, Ep. v. 6; Col. ii. 8; *empty-handed*, Lu. i. 53; Ja. ii. 20; *fruitless, ineffectual*, 1 Cor. xv. 10, 58. *Syn.:* κενός, *empty*, refers to the contents; μάταιος, *aimless, purposeless*, to the result.

κλέπτης, ου, ὁ, *a thief*, as Mat. vi. 19; met., of false teachers, Jn. x. 8. *Syn.:* κλέπτης, a thief, who steals *secretly;* λῃστής, a robber, who plunders *openly, by violence.*

λαλέω, ῶ, ήσω, (1) *to utter a sound, to speak*, absolutely, Rev. x. 4; Heb. xii. 24; Ja. ii. 12; (2) *to speak, to talk*, with acc. of thing spoken, also with modal dat. and dat. of person addressed. Hence, according to the nature of the case, met., *to declare*, by other methods than *vivâ voce*, as Ro. vii. 1; *to preach, to publish, to announce. Syn.:* λέγω has reference to the *thought* uttered; λαλέω simply to the *fact* of utterance.

λαμπάς, άδος, ἡ, prop. *a torch*, Rev. iv. 5, viii. 10; also *a lamp*, Jn. xviii. 3. *Syn.:* φῶς is light in general; φέγγος, radiance; φωστήρ, a heavenly body, luminary; λαμπάς, a torch; λύχνος, a lamp.

λατρεύω, σω, (1) *to worship, to serve*, Ac. vii. 7; (2) *to officiate as a priest*, Heb. xiii. 10. *Syn.:* λατρεύω is to worship God, as any one may do; λειτουργέω, to serve him in a special office or ministry.

λούω, σω, *to bathe, to wash*, Ac. ix. 37, xvi. 33; *to cleanse, to purify*, Rev. i. 5 (W. H. λύω). *Syn.:* πλύνω is to wash *inanimate things;* λούω, to bathe *the whole body;* νίπτω, to wash a *part* of the body.

μετα-μέλομαι, μελήσομαι, 1st aor. μετεμελήθην, dep., pass., *to change one's mind*, Mat. xxi. 30, 32; Heb. vii. 21; *to repent, to feel sorrow for, regret*, Mat. xxvii. 3; 2 Cor. vii. 8. *Syn.:* μετανοέω is the nobler word, the regular expression for thorough repentance; μεταμέλομαι is more loosely used, generally expressing sorrow, regret or remorse.

πένης, ητος, ὁ, *poor*, 2 Cor. ix. 9.* *Syn.:* πτωχός implies utter destitution, usually beggary; πένης, simply poverty, scanty livelihood.

πλεονεξία, ας, ἡ, *covetousness, avarice*, Lu. xii. 15; 2 Pet. ii. 3. *Syn.:* πλεονεξία is more active, seeking to grasp the things it has not; φιλαργυρία, more passive, seeking to retain and multiply what it has.

σπαταλάω, ῶ, ήσω, *to live extravagantly* or *luxuriously*, 1 Tim. v. 6; Ja. v. 5.* *Syn.:* The fundamental thought of στρηνιάω is of insolence and voluptuousness which spring from abundance; of τρυφάω, *effeminate* self-indulgence; of σπαταλάω, is effeminacy and wasteful extravagance.

SYNONYM DISTINCTIONS

ὕμνος, ου, ὁ, *a hymn, a sacred song*, Ep. v. 19; Col. iii. 16.* *Syn.:* ψαλμός is used of the Psalms of the O. T.; ὕμνος designates a song of *praise to God;* ᾠδή is a general expression for a song.

φέρω, οἴσω, ἤνεγκα, ἠνέχθην (see Gr. § 103, Wi. § 15, Bu. 68), *to bear*, as (1) *to carry*, as a burden, Lu. xxiii. 26; (2) *to produce* fruit, Jn. xii. 24; (3) *to bring*, Ac. v. 16; (4) *to endure, to bear with*, Ro. ix. 22; (5) *to bring forward*, as charges, Jn. xviii. 29; (6) *to uphold*, Heb. i. 3; (7) pass., as nautical term, *to be borne along*, Ac. xxvii. 15, 17, (8) mid., *to rush* (bear itself on), Ac. ii. 2; *to go on* or *advance*, in learning, Heb. vi. 1. *Syn.:* φορέω means to bear something habitually and continuously, while in φέρω it is temporary bearing, and on special occasions.

PART 2
Index to Synonym Distinctions

*This index includes only the synonyms discussed by Berry. The letter **a** represents the left-hand column in the lexical material and the letter **b**, the right-hand column.*

INDEX TO SYNONYM DISTINCTIONS

A	PAGES	SECT.
ἀγαθωσύνη	35a	
ἀγαπάω	35a, 24	31
ἅγιος	13	1
ἀγνόημα	13	2
ἁγνός	13	1
ἀγράμματος	35a	
ἄδολος	13	3
αἰδώς	15	5
αἵρεσις	25	33
αἰσχρολογία	14	4
αἰσχύνη	15	5
αἰτέω	35a, 26	37
αἰτία	16	7
αἴτημα	16	6
αἰών	35a, 26	38
ἄκακος	13	3
ἀκέραιος	13	3
ἀλαζών	16	8
ἀλείφω	35b	
ἀληθής	35b	
ἀληθινός	35b	
ἄλλος	35b	
ἀμαράντινος	17	9
ἀμάραντος	17	9
ἁμάρτημα	13	2
ἁμαρτία	13	2
ἄμεμπτος	17	10
ἀμίαντος	20	19
ἀμφίβληστρον	35b	
ἄμωμος	17	10
ἀνάθεμα	35b	
ἀνάθημα	36a	
ἀνακαίνωσις	17	10
ἀνάπαυσις	26	39
ἀνέγκλητος	17	10
ἄνεμος	27	40
ἀνεπίληπτος	17	10
ἄνεσις	26	39
ἀνθρωποκτόνος	18	12
ἀνομία	13	2
ἀνοχή	36a	
ἀντίτυπος	26	36
ἀντίχριστος	18	13
ἁπλοῦς	13	3
ἅπτομαι	36a	
ἄρτιος	36a	
ἀρχαῖος	27	41

	PAGES	SECT.
ἀρχιτελώνης	32	59
ἀσέβεια	13	2
ἀσέλγεια	18	14
ἄσπονδος	19	15
ἀστεῖος	19	16
ἀσύνθετος	19	15
ἀσωτία	18	14
αὐστηρός	27	42
ἄφεσις	36a	
ἄφθαρτος	17	9
ἀχλύς	27	43

B		
βίος	36a	
βόσκω	36b	
βούλομαι	24	32
βωμός	36b	

Γ		
γνόφος	28	43
γνῶσις	19	17

Δ		
δέησις	16	6
δεῖ	32	57
δειλία	36b	
δεισιδαίμων	20	18
δεσπότης	36b	
δημιουργός	36b	
δῆμος	28	44
διάδημα	36b	
διάκονος	28	45
διάνοια	25	34
δίδραχμον	32	58
δίκτυον	35b	
δόγμα	25	35
δοκέω	36b	
δοκιμάζω	37a	
δολόω	29	46
δοῦλος	28	45
δύναμις	37a	

E		
Ἑβραῖος	37a	
ἔθνος	28	44

43

INDEX TO SYNONYM DISTINCTIONS

	PAGES	SECT.
εἰλικρινής	20	19
ἐκκλησία	21	20
ἔλεγχος	16	7
ἐλέγχω	16	7
ἔλεος	24	30
ἑλκύω	37b	
Ἑλληνιστής	37a	
ἔντευξις	16	6
ἐντολή	25	35
ἐντροπή	15	5
ἐπίγνωσις	19	17
ἐπιείκεια	21	22
ἐπιθυμία	22	23
ἐπιτιμάω	16	7
ἐρωτάω	35a, 26	37
ἕτερος	35b	
εὐλάβεια	36b	
εὐλαβής	20	18
εὐσεβής	20	18
εὐτραπελία	14	4
εὐχαριστία	16	6
εὐχή	16	6

	PAGES	SECT.
Z		
ζόφος	28	43
ζωή	36a	
ζῶον	29	47

	PAGES	SECT.
H		
ἥττημα	13	2

	PAGES	SECT.
Θ		
θάλασσα	29	48
θειότης	37b	
θέλω	24	32
θεοσεβής	20	18
θεότης	37b	
θεράπων	28	45
θεσμός	25	35
θηρίον	29	47
θιγγάνω	36a	
θλῖψις	22	24
θρηνέω	29	49
θρῆσκος	20	18
θύελλα	27	40
θυμός	37b	

	PAGES	SECT.
θυσιαστήριον	36b	

	PAGES	SECT.
I		
ἰδέα	30	50
ἱερόν	37b	
ἱερός	13	1
ἱκετηρία	16	6
ἱμάτιον	30	51
ἱματισμός	30	51
Ἰουδαῖος	37a	
Ἰσραηλίτης	37a	

	PAGES	SECT.
K		
καθαρός	20	19
καινός	30	52
καιρός	37b	
κακός	22	25
καλός	19	16
καπηλεύω	29	46
κόλασις	23	26
κενός	38a	
κῆνσος	32	58
κλέπτης	38a	
κόπος	31	53
κόπτομαι	29	49
κόσμος	35b, 26	38
κόφινος	31	56
κραιπάλη	31	54
κύριος	36b	
κῶμος	31	54

	PAGES	SECT.
Λ		
λαῖλαψ	27	40
λαλέω	38a	
λαμπάς	38a	
λαός	28	44
λατρεύω	38a	
λέγω	38a	
λειτουργέω	38a	
λῃστής	38a	
λούω	38b	
λυπέομαι	29	49
λύχνος	38a	

INDEX TO SYNONYM DISTINCTIONS

M	PAGES	SECT.		PAGES	SECT.
μακροθυμία	36a		πάρεσις	36a	
μάταιος	38a		παροργισμός	37b	
μάχη	31	55	πατριά	33	61
μέθη	31	54	πειράζω	37a	
μεταμέλομαι	38b		πέλαγος	29	48
μετανοέω	38b		πένης	38b	
μιαίνω	23	27	πενθέω	29	49
μολύνω	23	27	πλεονεξία	38b	
μορφή	30	50	πλύνω	38b	
μόχθος	31	53	πνεῦμα	27	40
μωρολογία	14	4	πνοή	27	40
			ποδήρης	30	51
N			ποιέω	23	28
ναός	37b		ποιμαίνω	36b	
νέος	37b, 30	52	πόλεμος	31	55
νίπτω	38b		πονηρός	22	25
νόμος	25	35	πόνος	31	53
νοῦς	25	34	πότος	31	54
			πραότης	21	21 & 22
O			πράσσω	23	28
οἰκέτης	28	45	προσευχή	16	6
οἶκος	33	61	πτωχός	35a	
οἰκτιρμός	24	30	πυνθάνομαι	38b	
οἰνοφλυγία	31	54	Σ		
ὀλόκληρος	36a				
ὀργή	37b		σαγήνη	35b	
ὄρεξις	22	23	σαρκικός	23	29
ὁρμή	22	23	σάρκινος	23	29
ὅσιος	13	1	σεμνός	13	1
ὀφείλει	32	57	σημεῖον	37a	
ὄχλος	28	44	σικάριος	18	12
			σκληρός	27	42
Π			σκότος	28	43
πάθος	22	23	σοφία	19	17
παιδάριον	33	60	σπαταλάω	38b	
παιδίον	33	60	σπυρίς	31	56
παιδίσκη	33	60	στενοχωρία	22	24
παῖς	33	60	στέφανος	36b	
παλαιός	27	41	στολή	30	51
παλιγγενεσία	17	11	στρηνιάω	38b	
πανήγυρις	21	20	συναγωγή	21	20
παράβασις	13	2	σύρω	37b	
παρακοή	13	2	σχῆμα	30	50
παρανομία	13	2	σχίσμα	25	33
παράπτωμα	13	2	σωφροσύνη	15	5

45

INDEX TO SYNONYM DISTINCTIONS

T	PAGES	SECT.
ταπεινοφροσύνη	21	21
τέκνον	33	60
τέλειος	36a	
τέλος	32	58
τελώνης	32	59
τέρας	37a	
τεχνίτης	36b	
τιμωρία	23	26
τρυφάω	38b	
τύπος	26	36

Ψ	PAGES	SECT.
ψαλμός	39a	
ψευδόχριστος	18	13
ψηλαφάω	36a	
ψυχικός	23	29

Ω		
ᾠδή	39a	
ὡραῖος	19	16

Υ

ὑβιστής	16	8
υἱός	33	60
ὕμνος	39a	
ὑπερήφανος	16	8
ὑπηρέτης	28	45
ὑπομονή	36a	

Φ

φαίνομαι	37a	
φαῦλος	22	25
φέγγος	38a	
φέρω	39a	
φιλαργυρία	38b	
φιλέω	24	31
φόβος	36b	
φονεύς	18	12
φορέω	39a	
φόρος	32	58
φρόνησις	19	17
φυλή	33	61
φῶς	38a	
φωστήρ	38a	

Χ

χιτών	30	51
χλαμύς	30	51
χρηστότης	35a	
χρίω	35b	
χρόνος	37b	

PART 3
Synonym Groupings With Index to Bauer's *Greek-English Lexicon*

This section includes all the synonym groupings in both Trench and Berry.

SYNONYM GROUPINGS

A

ἀγαθός	2
καλός	400
ἀστεῖος	117
ὡραῖος	896

ἀγαθωσύνη	3
χρηστότης	886

ἀγαλλίασις	3
εὐφροσύνη	328
χαρά	875

ἀγαπάω	4
φιλέω	859

ἅγιος	9
ἁγνός	11
ἱερός	372
ὅσιος	585
σεμνός	746

ἁγνόημα	11
ἁμάρτημα	42
ἁμαρτία	43
ἀνομία	71
ἀσέβεια	114
ἥττημα	349
παράβασις	611
παρακοή	618
παρανομία	621
παράπτωμα	621

ἄγνοια	11
ἀγνωσία	12

ἁγνός	11
ἅγιος	9
ἱερός	372
ὅσιος	585
σεμνός	746

ἀγνωσία	12
ἄγνοια	11

ἀγράμματος	13
ἰδιώτης	370

ἀγωνίζομαι	15
κοπιάω	443

ᾅδης	16
γέεννα	153
τάρταρος *	
φυλακή	867

ἄδολος	18
ἄκακος	29
ἀκέραιος	30
ἁπλοῦς	86

ἀΐδιος	
αἰώνιος	22
	28

αἰδώς	22
αἰσχύνη	25
ἐντροπή	269
σωφροσύνη	802

αἵρεσις	23
σχίσμα	797

αἰσχρολογία	25
εὐτραπελία	327
μωρολογία	531

αἰσχύνη	25
αἰδώς	22
ἐντροπή	269
σωφροσύνη	802

αἰτέω	25
ἐρωτάω	311
πυνθάνομαι	729

αἰτία	26
ἔλεγχος	249
ἐλέγχω	249
ἐπιτιμάω	303

αἴτημα	26
δέησις	171
ἔντευξις	268
εὐχαριστία	328
εὐχή	329

* see τάρταρόω 805

49

SYNONYM GROUPINGS

ἱκετηρία	375
προσευχή	713
αἰών	27
κόσμος	445
αἰώνιος	28
ἀΐδιος	22
ἄκακος	29
ἄδολος	18
ἀκέραιος	30
ἁπλοῦς	86
ἀκέραιος	30
ἄδολος	18
ἄκακος	29
ἁπλοῦς	86
ἀλαζών	34
ὑβριστής	832
ὑπερήφανος	841
ἀλείφω	35
χρίω	887
ἀληθής	36
ἀληθινός	37
ἀληθινός	37
ἀληθής	36
ἀλληγορούμενον *	
ἀντίτυπος	76
τύπος	829
ὑπογραμμός	843
ὑπόδειγμα	844
ὑποτύπωσις	848
ἄλλος	39
ἕτερος	315
ἅλυσις	41
πέδη	638
ἀμαράντινος	42
ἀμάραντος	42
ἄφθαρτος	125

ἀμάραντος	42
ἀμαράντινος	42
ἄφθαρτος	125
ἁμάρτημα	42
ἀγνόημα	11
ἁμαρτία	43
ἀνομία	71
ἀσέβεια	114
ἥττημα	349
παράβασις	611
παρακοή	618
παρανομία	621
παράπτωμα	621
ἁμαρτία	43
ἀγνόημα	11
ἁμάρτημα	42
ἀνομία	43
ἀσέβεια	71
ἥττημα	114
παράβασις	349
παρακοή	611
παρανομία	618
παράπτωμα	621
ἄμεμπτος	45
ἄμωμος	47
ἀνέγκλητος	64
ἀνεπίλημπτος	65
ἀμετακίνητος	45
ἑδραῖος	217
τεθεμελιωμένος *	
ἀμίαντος	46
εἰλικρινής	240
καθαρός	388
ἀμνός	46
ἀρνίον	108
ἀμφίβληστρον	47
δίκτυον	198
σαγήνη	739

* see ἀλληγορέω 39

* see θεμελιόω 356

SYNONYM GROUPINGS

ἄμωμος	47
ἄμεμπτος	45
ἀνέγκλητος	64
ἀνεπίληπτος	65
ἀναβοάω	51
βοάω	144
κράζω	447
κραυγάζω	449
ἀνάθεμα	54
ἀνάθημα	54
ἀνάθημα	54
ἀνάθεμα	54
ἀνακαίνωσις	55
παλιγγενεσία	606
ἀνάμνησις	58
ὑπόμνησις	846
ἀνάπαυσις	58
ἄνεσις	65
κατάπαυσις	415
ἀνέγκλητος	64
ἄμεμπτος	45
ἄμωμος	47
ἀνεπίληπτος	65
ἄνεμος	64
θύελλα	365
λαῖλαψ	462
πνεῦμα	674
πνοή	680
ἀνεπίλημπτος	65
ἄμεμπτος	64
ἄμωμος	45
ἀνέγκλητος	47
ἄνεσις	65
ἀνάπαυσις	58
κατάπαυσις	415
ἄνευ	65
χωρίς	890
ἀνθρωποκτόνος	68
σικάριος	750
θονεύς	864
ἄνοια	70
ἀφροσύνη	127
μωρία	531
ἀνομία	71
ἀγνόημα	11
ἁμάρτημα	42
ἁμαρτία	43
ἀσέβεια	114
ἥττημα	349
παράβασις	611
παρακοή	618
παρανομία	621
παράπτωμα	621
ἀνοχή	72
μακροθυμία	488
ὑπομονή	846
ἀντί	73
ὑπέρ	838
ἀντίδικος	74
ἐχθρός	331
ὑπεναντίος	838
ἀντίτυπος	76
ἀλληγορούμενον*	
τύπος	829
ὑπογραμμός	843
ὑπόδειγμα	844
ὑποτύπωσις	848
ἀντίχριστος	76
ψευδόχριστος	892
ἀπατάω	81
παραλογίζομαι	620
πλανάω	665
ἀπειθής	82
ἄπιστος	85
ἄπιστος	85
ἀπειθής	82

* see ἀλληγορέω 39

SYNONYM GROUPINGS

ἁπλοῦς	86	ἀρχιτελώνης	113
ἄδολος	18	τελώνης	812
ἄκακος	29		
ἀκέραιος	30	ἀσέβεια	114
		ἀγνόημα	11
ἀποθήκη	91	ἁμάρτημα	42
γάζα	149	ἁμαρτία	43
θησαυρός	361	ἀνομία	71
ταμιεῖον	803	ἥττημα	349
		παράβασις	611
ἀποκάλυψις	92	παρακόη	618
ἐπιφάνεια	304	παρανομία	621
φανέρωσις	853	παράπτωμα	621
ἀποκαραδοκία	92		
ἐλπίς	252	ἀσέλγεια	114
		ἀσωτία	119
ἀπολύτρωσις	96		
ἱλασμός	375	ἀσθενής	115
καταλλαγή	414	ἄῤῥωστος	109
ἀποστέλλω	98	ἀσθένεια	115
πέμπω	641	μαλακία	488
		μάστιξ	495
ἅπτω	102	νόσος	543
θιγγάνω	361		
ψηλαφάω	892	ἄσπονδος	117
		ἀσύνθετος	118
ἀπώλεια	103		
ὄλεθρος	563	ἀστεῖος	117
		ἀγαθός	2
ἀργός	104	καλός	400
βραδύς	147	ὡραῖος	896
νωθρός	547		
		ἀσύνθετος	118
ἀρνίον	108	ἄσπονδος	117
ἀμνός	46		
		ἀσωτία	119
ἄῤῥωστος	109	ἀσέλγεια	114
ἀσθενής	115		
		αὐθάδης	120
ἄρτι	110	φίλαυτος	859
νῦν	545		
		αὐστηρός	122
ἄρτιος	110	σκληρός	756
ὁλόκληρος	564		
τέλειος	809	ἄφεσις	125
		πάρεσις	626
ἀρχαῖος	111		
παλαιός	605		

SYNONYM GROUPINGS

ἄφθαρτος	125		βλασφημέω	142
ἀμαράντινος	42		κακολογέω	397
ἀμάραντος	42		λοιδορέω	479
			μέμφομαι	502
ἀφροσύνη	127		ὀνειδίζω	570
ἄνοια	70			
μωρία	531		βλέπω	143
			θεάομαι	353
ἀχλύς	128		θεωρέω	360
γνόφος	163		ὀπτάνομαι	576
ζόφος	339		ὁράω	577
σκότος	757			
			βοάω	144
ἀχρεῖος	128		ἀναβοάω	51
ἄχρηστος	128		κράζω	447
			κραυγάζω	449
ἄχρηστος	128			
ἀχρεῖος	128		βοηθέω	144
			συλλαμβάνω	776
B				
			βόρβορος	145
βάπτισμα	132		πηλός	656
βαπτισμός	132			
			βόσκω	145
Βαπτισμός	132		ποιμαίνω	683
βάπτισμα	132			
			βούλομαι	146
βάρος	133		θέλω	354
ὄγκος	553			
φορτίον	865		βουνός	146
			ὄρος	582
βεβαιόω	138			
ῥιζοῦμαι*			βραδύς	147
			ἀργός	104
βέβηλος	138		νωθρός	547
κοινός	438			
			βρέφος	147
Βία	140		παιδάριον	603
δύναμις	207		παιδίον	604
ἐνέργεια	265		παιδίσκη	604
ἐξουσία	277		παῖς	604
ἰσχύς	383		τέκνον	808
κράτος	449		υἱός	833
βίος	141		βωμός	148
ζωή	340		θυσιαστήριον	366

* see ῥιζόω 736

SYNONYM GROUPINGS

Γ	
γάζα	149
ἀποθήκη	91
θησαυρός	361
	803

γέεννα	153
ᾄδης	16
τάρταρος*	
φυλακή	867

γέρων	157
πρεσβύτης	700

γινώσκω	160
γνωρίζω	163
ἐπιγινώσκω	291
ἐπίσταμαι	300
οἶδα	555

γλῶσσα	162
διάλεκτος	185

γνόφος	163
ἀχλύς	128
ζόφος	339
σκότος	757

γνωρίζω	163
γινώσκω	160
ἐπιγινώσκω	291
ἐπίσταμαι	300
οἶδα	555

γνῶσις	163
ἐπίγνωσις	291
σοφία	759
φρόνησις	866

γραμματεύς	165
νομικός	541
νομοδιδάσκαλος	541

Δ

δαιμόνιον	169
δαίμων	169
διάβολος	182
κατήγωρ	423

*see ταρταρόω 805

δαίμων	169
δαιμόνιον	169
διάβολος	182
κατήγωρ	423

δέησις	171
αἴτημα	26
ἔντευξις	268
εὐχαριστία	328
εὐχή	329
ἱκετηρία	375
προσευχή	713

δεῖ	172
ὀφειλή	598

δειλία	173
εὐλάβεια	321
φόβος	863

δεισιδαίμων	173
εὐλαβής	322
εὐσεβής	326
θεοσεβής	358
θρησκός	363

δεσμωτήριον	176
φυλακή	867

δεσπότης	176
κύριος	458

δημιουργός	178
τεχνίτης	814

δῆμος	179
ἔθνος	218
λαός	466
ὄχλος	600

διάβολος	182
δαιμόνιον	169
δαίμων	169
κατήγωρ	423

διάδημα	182
στέφανος	767

SYNONYM GROUPINGS

διάκονος	184
δοῦλος	205
θεράπων	359
οἰκέτης	557
ὑπηρέτης	842
εἰάλεκτος	185
γλῶσσα	162
διαλογισμός	186
ἐνθύμησις	266
ἔννοια	267
διάνοια	187
νοῦς	544
πνεῦμα	674
διδασκαλία	191
ἔνταλμα	268
διδάσκω	192
νουθετέω	544
σωφρονίζω	802
δίδραχμον	192
κῆνσος	430
τέλος	811
φόρος	865
διεστραμμένος	194
σκολιός	756
δικαιοσύνη	196
δικαίωμα	198
δικαίωσις	198
δικαίωμα	198
δικαιοσύνη	196
δικαίωσις	198
δικαίωσις	198
δικαιοσύνη	196
δικαίωμα	198
δικτυον	198
ἀμφίβληστρον	47
σαγήνη	739
δόγμα	201
ἐντολή	269
νόμος	542
παραγγελία	613

δοκέω	201
φαίνομαι*	
δοκιμάζω	202
πειράζω	640
δολόω	203
καπηλεύω	403
δόξα	203
ἔπαινος	281
τιμή	817
δοῦλος	205
διάκονος	184
θεράπων	359
οἰκέτης	557
ὑπηρέτης	842
δύναμις	207
ἔνδοξος	263
θαυμάσιος	352
μεγαλεῖος	496
παράδοξος	615
σημεῖον	747
τέρας	812
δύναμις	207
βία	140
ἐνέργεια	265
ἐξουσία	277
ἰσχύς	383
κράτος	449
δῶρον	210
θυσία	366
προσφορά	720

E

Ἑβραῖος	213
Ἑλληνιστής	252
Ἰουδαῖος	379
Ἰσραηλίτης	381

* see φαίνω 851

SYNONYM GROUPINGS

ἑδραῖος	217	ἐλπίς	252
ἀμετακίνητος	45	ἀποκαραδοκία	92
τεθεμελιωμένος*			
ἔθνος	218	ἔνδοξος	263
δῆμος	179	δύναμις	207
λαός	466	θαυμάσιος	352
ὄχλος	600	μεγαλεῖος	496
		παράδοξος	615
εἰκών	222	σημεῖον	747
ὁμοίωμα	567	τέρας	812
εἰλικρινής	222	ἐνέργεια	265
ἀμίαντος	46	βία	140
καθαρός	388	δύναμις	207
		ἐξουσία	277
ἐκκλησία	240	ἰσχύς	383
πανήγυρις	607	κράτος	449
συναγωγή	782		
		ἐνθύμησις	266
ἔκστασις	245	διαλογισμός	186
θάμβος	350	ἔννοια	267
πτόησις	727		
		ἔννοια	267
ἔλαιον	248	διαλογισμός	186
μύρον	529	ἐνθύμησις	266
ἔλεγχος	249	ἔνταλμα	268
αἰτία	26	διδασκαλία	191
ἐλέγχω	249		
ἐπιτιμάω	303		
		ἔντευξις	268
ἐλέγχω	249	αἴτημα	26
αἰτία	26	δέησις	171
ἔλεγχος	249	εὐχαριστία	328
ἐπιτιμάω	303	εὐχή	329
		ἱκετηρία	375
ἔλεος	250	προσευχή	713
οἰκτιρμός	561		
χάρις	877	ἐντολή	269
		δόγμα	201
ἕλκω	251	νόμος	542
σύρω	794	παραγγελία	613
Ἑλληνιστής	252	ἐντροπή	269
Ἑβραῖος	213	αἰδώς	22
Ἰουδαῖος	379	αἰσχύνη	25
Ἰσραηλίτης	381	σωφροσύνη	802

* see θεμελιόω 356

SYNONYM GROUPINGS

ἐξουσία	277		ἐριθεία	309
βία	140		ἔρις	309
δύναμις	207			
ἐνέργεια	265		ἔρις	309
ἰσχύς	383		ἐριθεία	309
κράτος	449			
			ἔρχομαι	310
ἔπαινος	281		ἥκω	344
δόξα	203			
τιμή	817		ἐρωτάω	311
			αἰτέω	25
ἐπιγινώσκω	291		πυνθάνομαι	729
γινώσκω	160			
γνωρίζω	163		ἐσθίω	312
ἐπίσταμαι	300		τρώγω	829
οἶδα	555		φάγομαι *	
ἐπίγνωσις	291		ἕτερος	315
γνῶσις	163		ἄλλος	39
σοφία	759			
φρόνησις	866		εὐλάβεια	321
			δειλία	173
ἐπιείκεια	292		φόβος	863
πραότης*				
			εὐλαβής	322
ἐπιθυμία	293		δεισιδαίμων	173
ὄρεξις	580		εὐσεβής	326
ὀρμή	581		θεοσεβής	359
πάθος	602		θρῆσκος	363
ἐπίσταμαι	300		εὐλογέω	322
γινώσκω	160		εὐχαριστέω	328
οἶδα	555			
			εὐμετάδοτος	323
ἐπιτιμάω	303		κοινωνικός	439
αἰτία	26			
ἔλεγχος	249		εὐσεβής	326
ἐλέγχω	249		δεισιδαίμων	173
			εὐλαβης	322
ἐπίτροπος	303		θεοσεβής	358
οἰκονόμος	560		θρήσκος	363
ἐπιφάνεια	304		εὐτραπελία	327
ἀποκάλυψις	92		αἰσχρολογία	25
φανέρωσις	853		μωρολογία	531

* see πραΰτης 669

* see ἐσθίω 312

57

SYNONYM GROUPINGS

εὐφροσύνη	328
ἀγαλλίασις	3
χαρά	875
εὐχαριστέω	328
εὐλογέω	322
εὐχαριστία	328
αἴτημα	26
δέησις	171
ἔντευξις	268
εὐχή	329
ἱκετηρία	375
προσευχή	713
εὐχή	329
αἴτημα	26
δέησις	171
ἔντευξις	268
εὐχαριστία	328
ἱκετηρία	375
προσευχή	713
ἐχθρός	331
ἀντίδικος	74
ὑπεναντίος	838

H

ἥκω	344
ἔρχομαι	310
ἤρεμος	348
ἡσύχιος	349
πραΰς	698
ἡσύχιος	349
ἤρεμος	348
πραΰς	698
ἥττημα	349
ἀγνόημα	11
ἁμάρτημα	42
ἁμαρτία	43
ἀνομία	71
ἀσέβεια	114
παράβασις	611
παρακοή	618
παρανομία	621
παράπτωμα	621

Z

ζῆλος	337
φθόνος	857
ζόφος	339
γνόφος	163
ἀχλύς	128
σκότος	757
ζωή	340
βίος	141
ζῷον	341
θηρίον	361

Θ

θάλασσα	350
πέλαγος	641
θάμβος	350
ἔκστασις	245
πτόησις	727
θαυμάσιος	352
δύναμις	207
ἔνδοξος	263
μεγαλεῖος	496
παράδοξος	615
σημεῖον	747
τέρας	812

SYNONYM GROUPINGS

θεάομαι	353		θιγγάνω	361
βλέπω	143		ἅπτω	102
θεωρέω	360		ψηλαφάω	892
ὀπτάνομαι	576			
ὁράω	577		θλῖψις	362
			στενοχωρία	766
θειότης	354			
θεότης	358		θνητός	362
			νεκρός	534
θέλω	354			
βούλομαι	146		θρηνέω	363
			κόπτομαι*	
θεμελιόω	356		λυπέομαι †	
στηρίζω	768		πενθέω	642
θεοσεβής	358		θρῆσκος	363
δεισιδαίμω	173		δεισιδαίμων	173
εὐλαβής	322		εὐλαβής	322
εὐσεβής	326		εὐσεβής	326
θρῆσκος	363		θεοσεβής	359
θεότης	358		θρίξ	363
θειότης	354		κόμη	442
θεραπεύω	359		θύελλα	365
ἰάομαι	368		ἄνεμος	64
			λαῖλαψ	462
θεράπων	359		πνεῦμα	674
διάκονος	184		πνοή	680
δοῦλος	205			
οἰκέτης	557		θυμός	365
ὑπηρέτης	842		ὀργή	578
			παροργισμός	629
θεωρέω	360			
βλέπω	143		θύρα	365
θεάομαι	353		πύλη	729
ὀπτάνομαι	576			
ὁράω	577		θυσία	366
			δῶρον	210
θηρίον	316		προσφορά	720
ζῷον	341			
			θυσιαστήριον	366
θησαυρός	361		βωμός	148
ἀποθήκη	91			
γάζα	149		* see κόπτω 444	
ταμιεῖον	803		† see λυπέω 481	

59

SYNONYM GROUPINGS

I

ἰάομαι	368
θεραπεύω	359
ἰδέα	369
μορφή	528
σχῆμα	797
ἰδιώτης	370
ἀγράμματος	13
ἱερόν	372
ναός	533
ἱεροπρεπής	372
κόσμιος	445
σεμνός	746
ἱερός	372
ἅγιος	9
ἁγνός	11
ὅσιος	585
σεμνός	746
ἱκετηρία	375
αἴτημα	26
δέησις	171
ἔντευξις	268
εὐχαριστία	328
εὐχή	329
προσευχή	713
ἱλασμός	375
ἀπολύτρωσις	96
καταλλαγή	414
ἱμάτιον	376
ἱματισμός	376
ποδήρης	680
στολή	769
χιτών	882
χλαμύς	882
ἱματισμός	376
ἱμάτιον	376
ποδήρης	680
στολή	769
χιτών	882
χλαμύς	882
Ἰουδαῖος	379
Ἑβραῖος	213
Ἑλληνιστής	252
Ἰσραηλίτης	381
Ἰσραηλίτης	381
Ἰουδαῖος	379
Ἑβραῖος	213
Ἑλληνιστής	252
ἰσχύς	383
βία	140
δύναμις	207
ἐνέργεια	265
ἐξουσία	277
κράτος	449

K

καθαρός	388
ἀμίαντος	46
εἰλικρινής	222
καινός	394
νέος	535
καιρός	394
χρόνος	887
κακία	397
κακοήθεια	397
κακοήθεια	397
κακία	397
κακός	397
πονηρός	690
φαῦλος	854
κακολογέω	397
βλασφημέω	142

SYNONYM GROUPINGS

λοιδορέω	479	κλέπτης	434
μέμφομαι	502	ληστής	473
ὀνειδίζω	570		
καλέω	398	κλίνη	436
ὀνομάζω	573	κράββατος	447
καπηλεύω	403	κλυδωνίζομαι	436
δολόω	203	περιφέρω	653
		ταράσσω	805
καταγινώσκω	409	τυρβάζω	830
κατακρίνω	412		
		κοινός	438
κατακρίνω	412	βέβηλος	138
καταγινώσκω	409		
		κοινωνικός	439
κατάλαλος	412	εὐμετάδοτος	323
ψιθυριστής	893		
		κοινωνός	439
καταλλαγή	414	μέτοχος	514
ἀπολύτρωσις	96		
ἱλασμός	375	κόλασις	440
		τιμωρία	818
κατάπαυσις	415		
ἀνάπαυσις	58	κόμη	442
ἄνεσις	65	θρίξ	363
καταρτίζω	417	κοπιάω	443
πληρόω	670	ἀγωνίζομαι	15
τελειόω	809		
		κόπος	443
κατήγωρ	423	μόχθος	528
δαιμόνιον	169	πόνος	691
δαίμων	169		
διάβολος	182	κόπτομαι*	
		θρηνέω	363
κειρία	427	λυπέομαι†	
ὀθόνη	555	πενθέω	642
κενός	427	κόσμιος	445
μάταιος	495	ἱεροπρεπής	372
		σεμνός	746
κῆνσος	430		
δίδραχμον	192	κόσμος	445
τέλος	811	αἰών	27
φόρος	865		
κῆπος	430	* see κόπτω 444	
παράδεισος	614	† see λυπέω 481	

61

SYNONYM GROUPINGS

κόφινος	447	Λ	
σπυρίς	764		
		λαῖλαψ	462
κράββατος	447	ἄνεμος	64
κλίνη	436	θύελλα	365
		πνεῦμα	674
κράζω	447	πνοή	680
βοάω	144		
ἀναβοάω	51	λαλέω	463
κραυγάζω	449	λέγω	468
κραιπάλη	448	λαλιά	464
κῶμος	461	λόγος	477
μέθη	498	μῦθος	529
οἰνοφλυγία	562	ῥῆμα	735
πότος	696	φωνή	870
κράτος	449		
βία	140	λαμπάς	
δύναμις	207	λύχνος	465
ἐνέργεια	265	φέγγος	483
ἐξουσία	277	φῶς	854
ἰσχύς	383	φωστήρ	871
			872
κραυγάζω	449	λαός	
ἀναβοάω	51	δῆμος	466
βοάω	144	ἔθνος	179
κράζω	447	ὄχλος	218
			600
κρέας	449	λατρεύω	467
σάρξ	743	λειτουργέω	470
κτῆμα	455		
ὕπαρξεις	837	λέγω	468
		λαλέω	463
κυβεία	456		
μεθοδεία	499	λειτουργέω	470
πανουργία	608	λατρεύω	467
κύριος	458	λῃστής	473
δεσπότης	176	κλέπτης	434
κῶμος	461	λόγος	477
κραιπάλη	448	λαλιά	464
μέθη	498	μῦθος	529
οἰνοφλυγία	562	ῥῆμα	735
πότος	696	φωνή	870

SYNONYM GROUPINGS

λοιδορέω	479		μάστιξ	495
βλασφημέω	142		ἀσθένεια	115
κακολογέω	397		μαλακία	488
μέμφομαι	502		νόσος	543
ὀνειδίζω	570			
			μάταιος	495
λούω	480		κενός	427
νίπτω	540			
πλύνω	674		μάχαιρα	496
			ῥομφαία	737
λυπέομαι*				
θρηνέω	363			
κόπτομαι†			μάχη	496
πενθέω	642		πόλεμος	685
λύπη	482			
ὀδύνη	555		μεγαλεῖος	496
ὠδίν	895		δύναμις	207
			ἔνδοξος	263
λυτρωτής	483		θαυμάσιος	352
σωτήρ	800		παράδοξος	615
			σημεῖον	747
λύχνος	483		τέρας	812
λαμπάς	465			
φέγγος	854		μέθη	498
φῶς	871		κραιπάλη	448
φωστήρ	872		κῶμος	461
			οἰνοφλυγία	562
			πότος	696
			μεθοδεία	499
M			κυβεία	456
			πανουργία	608
μακροθυμία	488			
ἀνοχή	72		μέμφομαι	502
ὑπομονή	846		βλασφημέω	142
			κακολογέω	397
μαλακία	488		λοιδορέω	479
ἀσθένεια	115		ὀνειδίζω	570
μάστιξ	495			
νόσος	543		μεριμνάω	505
			φροντίζω	866
μαντεύομαι	491			
προφητεύω	723		μεταμέλομαι	511
			μετανοέω	511
*see λυπέω 481			μετανοέω	511
†see κόπτω 444			μεταμέλομαι	511

63

SYNONYM GROUPINGS

μέτοχος	514	μωρολογία	531
κοινωνός	439	αἰσχρολογία	25
μετριοπαθέω	514	εὐτραπελία	327
συμπαθέω	778		
μιαίνω	520		
μολύνω	526	**N**	
μνημεῖον	524		
τάφος	806	ναός	533
		ἱερόν	372
μολύνω	526	νεκρός	534
μιαίνω	520	θνητός	362
μονή	527	νέος	535
οἰκία	557	καινός	394
μονογενής	527	νεφέλη	536
πρωτότοκος	726	νέφος	537
μορφή	528	νέφος	537
ἰδέα	369	νεφέλη	536
σχῆμα	797		
		νίπτω	540
μόχθος	528	λούω	480
κόπος	443	πλύνω	674
πόνος	691		
		νομικός	541
μῦθος	529	γραμματεύς	165
λαλιά	464	νομοδιδάσκαλος	541
λόγος	477		
ῥῆμα	735	νομοδιδάσκαλος	541
φωνή	870	γραμματεύς	165
		νομικός	541
μυκάομαι	529		
ὠρύομαι	897	νόμος	542
		δόγμα	201
μύρον	529	ἐντολή	269
ἔλαιον	247	παραγγελία	613
μώλωψ	531	νόσος	543
πληγή	668	ἀσθένεια	115
στίγμα	768	μαλακία	488
		μάστιξ	495
μωρία	531		
ἄνοια	70	νουθεσία	544
ἀφροσύνη	127	παιδεία	603

SYNONYM GROUPINGS

νουθετέω	544	οἰκέτης	557
διδάσκω	192	διάκονος	184
σωφρονίζω	802	δοῦλος	205
		θεράπων	359
νοῦς	544	ὑπηρέτης	842
διάνοια	187		
πνεῦμα	674	οἰκία	557
		μονή	527
νῦν	545		
ἄρτι	110	οἰκονόμος	560
		ἐπίτροπος	303
νωθρός	547		
ἀργός	104	οἶκος	560
βραδύς	147	πατρία	636
		φυλή	868
		οἰκτιρμός	561
		ἔλεος	250
Ξ			
		οἰνοφλυγία	562
ξένος	548	κραιπάλη	448
παρεπίδημος	625	κῶμος	461
πάροικος	629	μέθη	498
		πότος	696
ξύλον	547		
σταυρός	764	ὄλεθρος	563
		ἀπώλεια	103
		ὁλόκληρος	564
		ἄρτιος	110
Ο		τέλειος	809
ὄγκος	553	ὄμβρος	565
βάρος	133	ὑετός	833
φορτίον	865		
		ὄμμα	565
ὀδύνη	555	ὀφθαλμός	599
λύπη	482		
ὠδίν	895	ὁμοίωμα	567
		εἰκών	222
ὀθόνη	555		
κειρία	427	ὁμοίωσις	568
		παραβολή	612
οἶδα	555	παροιμία	629
γινώσκω	160		
γνωρίζω	163	ὀνειδίζω	570
ἐπίσταμαι	291	βλασφημέω	142
ἐπιγινώσκω	300	κακολογέω	397

65

SYNONYM GROUPINGS

λοιδορέω	479		ὄχλος	600
μέμφομαι	502		δῆμος	179
			ἔθνος	218
ὀνομάζω	573		λαός	466
καλέω	398			

Π

ὀπτάνομαι	576			
βλέπω	143			
θεάομαι	353			
θεωρέω	360		πάθος	602
ὁράω	577		ἐπιθυμία	293
			ὄρεξις	580
ὁράω	577		ὁρμή	581
βλέπω	143			
θεάομαι	353			
θεωρέω	360		παιδάριον	603
ὀπτάνομαι	576		βρέφος	147
			παιδίον	604
ὀργή	578		παιδίσκη	604
θυμός	365		παῖς	604
παροργισμός	629		τέκνον	808
			υἱός	833
ὄρεξις	580			
ἐπιθυμία	293		παιδεία	603
πάθος	602		νουθεσία	544
ὁρμή	581			
			παιδίον	604
ὁρμή	581		βρέφος	147
ἐπιθυμία	293		παιδάριον	603
πάθος	602		παιδίσκη	604
ὄρεξις	580		παῖς	604
			τέκνον	808
ὄρνεν	581		υἱός	833
πετεινόν	654			
			παιδίσκη	604
ὄρος	582		βρέφος	147
βουνός	146		παιδάριον	603
			παιδίον	604
ὅσιος	585		παῖς	604
ἅγιος	9		τέκνον	808
ἁγνός	11		υἱός	833
ἱερός	372			
σεμνός	746		παῖς	604
			βρέφος	147
ὀφειλή	598		παιδάριον	603
δεῖ	172		παιδίον	604
			παιδίσκη	604
ὀφθαλμός	599		τέκνον	808
ὄμμα	565		υἱός	833

SYNONYM GROUPINGS

παῖς θεοῦ	604		παράκλησις	618
υἱὸς θεοῦ	833		παραμυθία	620
παλαιός	605		παρηγορία	626
ἀρχαῖος	111		παρακοή	618
			ἀγνόημα	11
παλιγγενεσία	606		ἁμάρτημα	42
ἀνακαίνωσις	55		ἁμαρτία	43
			ἀνομία	71
πανήγυρις	607		ἀσέβεια	114
ἐκκλησία	240		ἥττημα	349
συναγωγή	782		παράβασις	611
			παρανομία	621
πανουργία	608		παράπτωμα	621
κυβεία	456		παραλογίζομαι	620
μεθοδεία	499		ἀπατάω	81
			πλανάω	665
παράβασις	611			
ἀγνόημα	11		παραμυθία	620
ἁμάρτημα	42		παρηγορία	626
ἁμαρτία	43		παράκλησις	618
ἀνομία	71			
ἀσέβεια	114		παρανομία	621
ἥττημα	349		ἀγνόημα	11
παρακοή	618		ἁμάρτημα	42
παρανομία	621		ἁμαρτία	53
παράπτωμα	621		ἀνομία	71
			ἀσέβεια	114
παραβολή	612		ἥττημα	349
ὁμοίωσις	568		παράβασις	611
παροιμία	629		παρακοή	618
			παράπτωμα	621
παραγγελία	613			
δόγμα	201		παράπτωμα	621
ἐντολή	269		ἀγνόημα	11
νόμος	542		ἁμάρτημα	42
			ἁμαρτία	53
παράδεισος	614		ἀνομία	71
κῆπος	430		ἀσέβεια	114
			ἥττημα	349
παράδοξος	615		παράβασις	611
δύναμις	207		παρακοή	618
ἔνδοξος	263		παρανομία	621
θαυμάσιος	352			
μεγαλεῖος	496		παρεπίδημος	625
σημεῖον	747		ξένος	548
τέρας	812		πάροικος	629

67

SYNONYM GROUPINGS

πάρεσις	626
ἄφεσις	125
παρηγορία	626
παραμυθία	620
παράκλησις	618
πάροικος	629
ξένος	548
παρεπίδημος	625
παροιμία	629
ὁμοίωσις	568
παραβολή	612
παροργισμός	629
θυμός	365
ὀργή	578
πατρία	636
οἶκος	560
φυλή	868
πέδη	638
ἅλυσις	41
πειράζω	640
δοκιμάζω	202
πέλαγος	641
θάλασσα	350
πέμπω	641
ἀποστέλλω	98
πένης	642
πτωχός	728
πενθέω	642
θρηνέω	363
κόπτομαι *	
λυπέομαι †	
περιφέρω	653
κλυδωνίζομαι	436
ταράσσω	805

*see κόπτω 444
†see λυπέω 481

τυρβάζω	830
πετεινόν	654
ὄρνεον	581
πηγή	655
φρέαρ	865
πηλός	656
βόρβορος	145
πικρία	657
χολή	883
πλανάω	665
ἀπατάω	81
παραλογίζομαι	620
πλεονεξία	667
φιλαργυρία	857
πληγή	668
μώλωψ	531
στίγμα	768
πληρόω	670
καταρτίζω	417
τελειόω	809
πλύνω	674
λούω	480
νίπτω	540
πνεῦμα	674
ἄνεμος	64
θύελλα	365
λαῖλαψ	462
πνοή	680
πνεῦμα	674
διάνοια	187
νοῦς	544
πνοή	680
ἄνεμος	64
θύελλα	365
λαῖλαψ	462
πνεῦμα	674

SYNONYM GROUPINGS

ποδήρης	680	πρεσβύτης	700
ἱμάτιον	376	γέρων	157
ἱματισμός	376		
στολή	769	προσευχή	713
χιτών	882	αἴτημα	26
χλαμύς	882	δέησις	171
		ἔντευξις	268
ποιέω	680	εὐχαριστία	328
πράσσω	698	εὐχή	329
		ἱκετηρία	375
ποιμαίνω	683		
βόσκω	145	προσφορά	720
		δῶρον	210
πόλεμος	685	θυσία	366
μάχη	496		
		προφητεύω	723
πονηρός	690	μαντεύομαι	491
κακός	397		
φαῦλος	854	πρωτότοκος	726
		μονογενής	527
πόνος	691		
κόπος	443	πτόησις	727
μόχθος	528	ἔκστασις	245
		θάμβος	350
ποταμός	694		
χείμαρρος	879	πτωχός	728
		πένης	642
πότος	696		
κραιπάλη	448	πύλη	729
κῶμος	461	θύρα	365
μέθη	498		
οἰνοφλυγία	562	πυνθάνομαι	729
		αἰτέω	25
πραότης*		ἐρωτάω	311
ἐπιείκεια	298		
		Ρ	
πραότης	698		
ταπεινοφροσύνη	804	ῥῆμα	735
		λαλία	464
πράσσω	698	λόγος	477
ποιέω	680	μῦθος	529
		φωνή	870
πραΰς	698		
ἤρεμος	348	ῥιζούμαι*	
ἡσύχιος	349	βεβαιόω	138

*see πραΰτης 699   *see ῥιζόω 736

69

SYNONYM GROUPINGS

ῥομφαία	737
μάχαιρα	496

Σ

σαγήνη	739
ἀμφίβληστρον	47
δίκτυον	198
σαρκικός	742
σάρκινος	742
ψυχικός	894
σάρκινος	742
σαρκικός	742
ψυχικός	894
σάρξ	743
κρέας	449
σεμνός	746
ἅγιος	9
ἁγνός	11
ἱερός	372
ὅσιος	585
σεμνός	746
ἱεροπρεπής	372
κόσμιος	445
σημεῖον	747
δύναμις	207
ἔνδοξος	263
θαυμάσιος	352
μεγαλεῖος	496
παράδοξος	615
τέρας	812
σιγάω	749
σιωπάω	752
σικάριος	750
ἀνθρωποκτόνος	68
φονεύς	864
σιωπάω	752
σιγάω	749

σκληρός	756
αὐστηρός	122
σκολιός	756
διεστραμμένος	194
σκότος	757
ἀχλύς	128
γνόφος	163
ζόφος	339
σοφία	759
γνῶσις	163
ἐπίγνωσις	291
φρόνησις	866
σπαταλάω	761
στρηνιάω	771
τρυφάω	828
σπυρίς	764
κόφινος	447
σταυρός	764
ξύλον	547
στενοχωρία	766
θλῖψις	362
στέφανος	767
διάδημα	182
στηρίζω	768
θεμελιόω	356
στίγμα	768
μώλωψ	531
πληγή	668
στολή	769
ἱμάτιον	376
ἱματισμός	376
ποδήρης	680
χιτών	882
χλαμύς	882
στρηνιάω	771
σπαταλάω	761
τρυφάω	828

SYNONYM GROUPINGS

συλλαμβάνω	776	τυρβάζω	830
βοηθέω	144		
συμπαθέω	778	ταρτάρος*	
μετριοπαθέω	514	ᾅδης	16
		γέεννα	153
συναγωγή	782	φυλακή	867
ἐκκλησία	240		
πανήγυρις	607	τάφος	806
		μνημεῖον	524
σύρω	794		
ἕλκω	251	τεθεμελεωμένος†	
		ἀμετακίνητος	45
σχῆμα	797	ἑδραῖος	217
ἰδέα	369		
μορφή	528	τέκνον	808
		βρέφος	147
σχίσμα	797	παιδάριον	603
αἵρεσις	23	παιδίον	604
		παιδίσκη	604
σωτήρ	800	παῖς	604
λυτρωτής	483	υἱός	833
σωφρονίζω	802	τέλειος	809
διδάσκω	192	ἄρτιος	110
νουθετέω	544	ὁλόκληρος	564
σωφροσύνη	802	τελειόω	809
αἰδώς	22	καταρτίζω	417
αἰσχύνη	25	πληρόω	670
ἐντροπή	269		
		τέλος	811
		δίδραχμον	192
T		κῆνσος	430
ταμιεῖον	803	φόρος	865
ἀποθήκη	91		
γάζα	149	τελώνης	812
θησαυρός	361	ἀρχιτελώνης	113
ταπεινοφροσύνη	804	τέρας	812
πραότης*		δύναμις	207
		ἔνδοξος	263
ταράσσω	805	θαυμάσιος	352
κλυδωνίζομαι	436	μεγαλεῖος	496
περιφέρω	653	παράδοξος	615
		σημεῖον	747

* see πραΰτης 699
* see ταρταρόω 805
† see θεμελιόω 356

71

SYNONYM GROUPINGS

τεχνίτης	814		υἱός	833
δημιουργός	178		βρέφος	147
			παιδάριον	603
τηρέω	814		παιδίον	604
φρουρέω	867		παιδίσκη	604
φυλάσσω	868		παῖς	604
			τέκνον	808
τιμή	817			
δόξα	203		υἱὸς θεοῦ	833
ἔπαινος	281		παῖς θεοῦ	604
τιμωρία	818		ὕμνος	836
κόλασις	440		ψαλμός	891
			ᾠδή	895
τρυφάω	828			
σπαταλάω	761		ὑπάρξεις	837
στρηνιάω	771		κτῆμα	455
τρώγω	829		ὑπεναντίος	838
ἐσθίω	312		ἀντίδικος	74
φάγομαι*	312		ἐχθρός	331
τύπος	829		ὑπέρ	838
ἀλληγορούμενον†			ἀντί	73
ἀντίτυπος	76			
ὑπογραμμός	843		ὑπερήφανος	841
ὑπόδειγμα	844		ἀλαζών	34
ὑποτύπωσις	848		ὑβριστής	832
τυρβάζω	830		ὑπηρέτης	842
κλυδωνίζομαι	436		διάκονος	184
περιφέρω	653		δοῦλος	205
ταράσσω	805		θεράπων	359
			οἰκέτης	557
			ὑπογραμμός	843
Υ			ἀλληγορούμενον*	
			ἀντίτυπος	76
ὑβριστής	832		τύπος	829
ἀλαζών	34		ὑπόδειγμα	844
ὑπερήφανος	841		ὑποτύπωσις	848
ὑετός	833			
ὄμβρος	565			

*see ἐσθίω 312
†see ἀλληγορέω 39

* see ἀλληγορέω 39

SYNONYM GROUPINGS

ὑπόδειγμα	844
ἀλληγορούμενον*	
ἀντίτυπος	76
τύπος	829
ὑπογραμμός	843
ὑποτύπωσις	848
ὑπόμνησις	846
ἀνάμνησις	58
ὑπομονή	846
ἀνοχή	72
μακροθυμία	488
ὑποτύπωσις	848
ἀλληγορούμενον*	
ἀντίτυπος	76
τύπος	829
ὑπογραμμός	843
ὑπόδειγμα	844
ὗς	848
χοῖρος	883

Φ

φάγομαι†	
ἐσθίω	312
τρώγω	829
φαίνομαι‡	
δοκέω	201
φανέρωσις	853
ἀποκάλυψις	92
ἐπιφάνεια	304
φαῦλος	854
κακός	397
πονηρός	690

φέγγος	854
λαμπάς	465
λύχνος	483
φῶς	871
φωστήρ	872
φέρω	854
φορέω	864
φθόνος	857
ζῆλος	337
φιλαργυρία	859
πλεονεξία	667
φίλαυτος	859
αὐθάδης	120
φιλέω	859
ἀγαπάω	4
φόβος	863
δειλία	173
εὐλάβεια	321
φονεύς	864
ἀνθρωποκτόνος	68
σικάριος	750
φορέω	864
φέρω	854
φόρος	865
δίδραχμον	192
κῆνσος	430
τέλος	811
φορτίον	865
βάρος	133
ὄγκος	553
φρέαρ	865
πηγή	655

---

* see ἀλληγορέω 39
† see ἐσθίω 312
‡ see φαίνω 851

SYNONYM GROUPINGS

φρόνησις	866		Χ	
γνῶσις	163			
ἐπίγνωσις	291		χαρά	875
σοφία	759		ἀγαλλίασις	3
			εὐφροσύνη	328
φροντίζω	866			
μεριμνάω	505		χάρις	877
			ἔλεος	250
φρουρέω	867		οἰκτιρμός	561
τηρέω	814			
φυλάσσω	868		χείμαρρος	879
			ποταμός	694
φυλακή	867			
ᾅδης	16		χιτών	882
γέεννα	153		ἱμάτιον	376
τάρταρος*			ἱματισμός	376
			ποδήρης	680
φυλακή	867		στολή	769
δεσμωτήριον	176		χλαμύς	882
φυλάσσω	868		χλαμύς	882
τηρέω	814		ἱμάτιον	376
φρουρέω	867		ἱματισμός	376
			ποδήρης	680
φυλή	868		στολή	769
οἶκος	560		χιτών	882
πατριά	636			
			χοῖρος	883
φωνή	870		ὗς	848
λαλιά	464			
λόγος	477		χολή	883
μῦθος	529		πικρία	657
ῥῆμα	735			
			χρηστότης	886
			ἀγαθωσύνη	3
φῶς	871			
λαμπάς	465		χρίω	887
λύχνος	483		ἀλείφω	35
φέγγος	854			
φωστήρ	872		χρόνος	887
			καιρός	394
φωστήρ	872			
λαμπάς	465		χωρίς	890
λύχνος	483		ἄνευ	65
φέγγος	854			
φῶς	871			

*see ταρταρόω 805

74

SYNONYM GROUPINGS

Ψ

ψαλμός	891
ὕμνος	836
ᾠδή	895
ψευδόχριστος	892
ἀντίχριστος	76
ψηλαφάω	892
ἅπτω	102
θιγγάνω	361
ψιθυριστής	893
κατάλαλος	412
ψυχικός	894
σάρκινος	742
σαρκικός	742

Ω

ᾠδή	895
ὕμνος	836
ψαλμός	891
ὠδίν	895
λύπη	482
ὀδύνη	555
ὡραῖος	896
ἀστεῖος	117
καλός	400
ὠρύομαι	897
μυκάομαι	529

PART 4
Synonym List With Index to Brown's
Dictionary of New Testament Theology

This section includes all the synonyms listed in Trench and Berry and should be used in conjunction with the synonym groups given in Part 3.

SYNONYM LIST

A

ἀγαθός
  Vol. 1: 348, 351, 561, 564; Vol. 2: 60, 98-106, 239, 241, 243, 403, 476, 683, 781, 846; Vol. 3: 45, 138, 775, 1148, 1158
ἀγαθωσύνη
  Vol. 2: 98, 100f., 819
ἀγαλλίασις
  Vol. 2: 352-354, 358
ἀγαπάω
  Vol. 2: 538-540, 542-544, 547-549, 551; Vol. 3: 173, 455, 942
ἅγιος
  Vol. 1: 105, 272, 275, 300, 305; Vol. 2:93, 223f., 227, 229, 231f., 237, 388, 547, 549, 653, 669, 673, 683, 826, 839, 868; Vol. 3: 38, 101, 104f., 107, 487, 491, 695, 774, 794, 814, 925, 1047, 1176-1178, 1210f.
ἀγνόημα
  Vol. 2: 406
ἄγνοια
  Vol. 1: 422; Vol. 2: 406f., 458; Vol. 3: 573, 577, 997
ἀγνός
  Vol. 1: 495; Vol. 3: 100-102
ἀγνωσία
  Vol. 1: 513; Vol. 2: 402, 406
ἀγράμματος
  Vol. 2: 456; Vol. 3: 1197
ἀγωνίζομαι
  Vol. 1: 644-647
ᾅδης
  Vol. 1: 264, 433, 463; Vol. 2:85, 188, 191, 205-210; Vol. 3: 262, 267, 388, 858, 947, 984
ἄδολος
  Vol. 3: 1118
ἀΐδιος
  Vol. 2: 290; Vol. 3: 826f., 829
αἰδώς
  Vol. 3: 561f., 564
αἵρεσις
  Vol. 1: 533-535; Vol. 3: 941
αἰσχρολογία
  Vol. 3: 564
αἰσχύνη
  Vol. 2: 212; Vol. 3: 561, 562-564

αἰτέω
  Vol. 2: 855-858, 859, 861, 868; Vol. 3: 683
αἴτημα
  Vol. 2: 855, 858, 861
αἰτία
  Vol. 2:137-139; Vol. 3:573
αἰών
  Vol. 1: 105, 125, 164, 179, 325f., 476, 523f., 601, 708, 718, 737; Vol. 2: 37, 62, 158, 543, 609, 887, 928; Vol. 3: 276, 312, 826-833, 841, 850, 864
αἰώνιος
  Vol. 1: 442, 464; Vol. 2:388, 480, 483, 928; Vol. 3: 98f., 199, 517, 812, 826f., 829f., 832, 844, 850, 1212
ἄκακος
  Vol. 1: 561, 563
ἀκέραιος
  no entry
ἀλαζών
  Vol. 2: 430, 435; Vol. 3: 28, 30-32
ἀλείφω
  Vol. 1: 119-121, 124, 471; Vol. 2: 335, 712f.; Vol. 3: 1060
ἀληθής
  Vol. 3: 874-877, 882-884, 888-891, 893
ἀληθινός
  Vol. 1: 98; Vol. 2: 280, 477, 724, 837, 878; Vol. 3: 874, 877, 883f., 888f., 891, 893
ἀλληγορούμενον
  See allegoreo Vol. 2: 743, 746, 755f., 760
ἄλλος
  Vol. 1: 666, 684, 691; Vol. 2: 423, 618, 739, 741f., 744, 785f.; Vol. 3: 166, 185, 1080, 1176
ἄλυσις
  no entry
ἀμαράντινος
  no entry
ἀμάραντος
  no entry
ἁμάρτημα
  Vol. 2:767; Vol. 3:577, 579

79

SYNONYM LIST

ἁμαρτία
Vol. 1: 86, 125, 160, 430, 446, 461, 562f., 682, 699, 701, 703, 733, 741; Vol. 2: 93f., 120, 411, 457, 460, 504, 533, 566, 668, 717; Vol. 3: 52, 55, 152, 161f., 168, 170f., 180, 243, 375, 419f., 434, 549, 573, 575-577, 579-582, 584, 587, 596f., 717, 811, 1178, 1197, 1203

ἄμεμπτος
Vol. 2: 137, 139, 143-145; Vol. 3: 348, 923-925

ἀμετακίνητος
no entry

ἀμίαντος
Vol. 1: 447f.; Vol. 3: 923, 925

ἀμνός
Vol. 2: 194, 410-414; Vol. 3: 611, 925

ἀμφίβληστρον
no entry

ἄμωμος
Vol. 2: 144; Vol. 3: 923-925

ἀναβοάω
Vol. 1: 410f.

ἀνάθεμα
Vol. 1: 413-415, 418; Vol. 2: 516, 520, 741, 896; Vol. 3: 171

ἀνάθημα
Vol. 1: 413f.

ἀνακαίνωσις
Vol. 1: 178, 185, 708; Vol. 2: 670, 673

ἀνάμνησις
Vol. 1: 370, 483; Vol. 2: 533, 717; Vol. 3: 230f., 238f., 241, 243-245, 247. 260

ἀνάπαυσις
Vol. 2: 281; Vol. 3: 254-256, 407

ἀνέγκλητος
Vol. 2: 137, 139; Vol. 3: 923-925, 932

ἄνεμος
Vol. 2: 155; Vol. 3: 690, 770, 1000f., 1198

ἀνεπίλημπτος
Vol. 3: 750

ἄνεσις
no entry

ἄνευ
no entry

ἀνθρωποκτόνος
no entry

ἄνοια
Vol. 3: 122f., 125, 128

ἀνομία
Vol. 1: 125, 556, 639; Vol. 2: 438, 440, 447-449, 709; Vol. 3: 137, 505, 573, 584, 717

ἀνοχή
Vol. 2: 765-767, 771

ἀντί
Vol. 1: 124, 400; Vol. 2: 119; Vol. 3: 195-197, 611, 1171f., 1174, 1179f., 1196f.

ἀντίδικος
Vol. 1: 553f.; Vol. 3: 173, 469

ἀντίτυπος
Vol. 3: 888, 903

ἀντίχριστος
Vol. 1: 124; Vol. 2: 435

ἀπατάω
Vol. 2: 457-461

ἀπειθής
Vol. 1: 558f., 593

ἄπιστος
Vol. 1: 594, 602; Vol. 2: 457

ἁπλοῦς
Vol. 2: 487, 744; Vol. 3: 571f.

ἀποθήκη
no entry

ἀποκάλυψις
Vol. 1: 50, 737; Vol. 2: 517; Vol. 3: 310f., 313-316, 502

ἀποκαραδοκία
Vol. 2: 238, 244-246; Vol. 3: 745

ἀπολύτρωσις
Vol. 1: 268, 301, 701; Vol. 2: 388, 839, 883; Vol. 3: 189f., 193, 199f.

ἀποστέλλω
Vol. 1: 126-128, 133f., 136, 332

ἅπτω
Vol. 1: 241; Vol. 3: 859f.

ἀπώλεια
Vol. 1: 462-466, 471; Vol. 2: 126; Vol. 3: 1187

ἀργός
Vol. 1: 73; Vol. 2: 96

SYNONYM LIST

ἀρνίον
Vol. 2: 410-413; Vol. 3: 568
ἄρρωστος
no entry
ἄρτι
Vol. 1: 282; Vol. 2: 756; Vol. 3: 409, 833f., 837, 850
ἄρτιος
Vol. 3: 348, 349f., 352
ἀρχαῖος
Vol. 1: 164f., 167, 508, 666; Vol. 2: 671, 713
ἀρχιτελώνης
Vol. 3: 755, 758
ἀσέβεια
Vol. 1: 622; Vol. 2: 91-94; Vol. 3: 49, 573, 576, 580, 584
ἀσέλγεια
Vol. 2: 587
ἀσθένεια
Vol. 3: 281, 993-996, 998, 1190
ἀσθενής
Vol. 2: 828; Vol. 3: 993-995, 1000
ἄσπονδος
no entry
ἀστεῖος
no entry
ἀσύνθετος
no entry
ἀσωτία
no entry
αὐθάδης
no entry
αὐστηρός
no entry
ἄφεσις
Vol. 1: 160, 697f., 700-703; Vol. 2: 533, 667; Vol. 3: 52, 55, 191, 1178, 1184
ἄφθαρτος
Vol. 1: 467f.; Vol. 3: 1201
ἀφροσύνη
Vol. 3: 1023-1026
ἀχλύς
no entry
ἀχρεῖος
no entry
ἄχρηστος
no entry

B

βάπτισμα
Vol. 1: 144, 146, 149f., 160, 703; Vol. 3: 52, 55
Βαπτισμός
Vol. 1: 144, 146, 149f.; Vol. 3: 770
βάρος
Vol. 1: 260f., 263
βεβαιόω
Vol. 1: 658f.; Vol. 3: 924
βέβηλος
no entry
Βία
Vol. 2: 601; Vol. 3: 574, 711, 925
βίος
Vol. 1: 460, 640; Vol. 2: 474f., 476-478, 845f.; Vol. 3: 32, 839, 935
βλασφημέω
Vol. 1: 413; Vol. 2: 143; Vol. 3: 340-342, 344, 346, 347, 364, 471, 473, 696
βλέπω
Vol. 1: 602, 713; Vol. 2: 142, 243, 488, 756, 914; Vol. 3: 126, 511f., 515, 517, 520
βοάω
Vol. 1: 410-412; Vol. 2: 855; Vol. 3: 53, 55, 118
βοηθέω
no entry
βόρβορος
Vol. 3: 679
βόσκω
Vol. 2: 210, 411
βούλομαι
Vol. 1: 533f., 569; Vol. 3: 1015-1018, 1019-1021, 1023
βουνός
no entry
βραδύς
no entry
βρέφος
Vol. 1: 160, 280f., 283f.
βωμός
Vol. 3: 418, 431

81

SYNONYM LIST

Γ

γάζα
no entry

γέεννα
Vol. 1: 231, 623; Vol. 2: 143, 205, 207, 208-210; Vol. 3: 110, 446

γέρων
Vol. 2: 674

γινώσκω
Vol. 1: 233, 245, 432, 484, 692, 716, 724; Vol. 2: 158, 202, 221, 390-408, 448, 460, 490, 586, 757; Vol. 3: 125, 168, 170, 205f., 310, 316, 630, 639, 679, 720, 835, 1031, 1199

γλῶσσα
Vol. 1: 143, 530; Vol. 2: 126, 505, 785f.; Vol. 3: 75, 180, 346, 505, 576, 770, 1078f., 1143, 1176

γωόφος
no entry

γνωρίζω
Vol. 3: 44, 310, 314

γνῶσις
Vol. 1: 58, 73, 422, 513, 708; Vol. 2: 219, 391, 392-406, 408, 477, 480, 539, 545, 646, 655, 677, 685; Vol. 3: 206, 310, 640, 647, 885, 932, 936, 996, 1201

γραμματεύς
Vol. 1: 199; Vol. 2: 714, 834; Vol. 3: 184, 477-480, 482

Δ

δαιμόνιον
Vol. 1: 450-452, 636f.; Vol. 2: 284, 520, 691; Vol. 3: 468, 473, 475

δαίμων
Vol. 1: 102, 168, 449-454; Vol. 2: 85, 498; Vol. 3: 473, 727

δέησις
Vol. 2: 855, 860f.; Vol. 3: 1174

δεῖ
Vol. 2: 139, 662-669, 808, 878, 912; Vol. 3: 39, 504, 624, 723, 957

δειλία
Vol. 1: 622

δεισιδαίμων
Vol. 1: 450, 453; Vol. 2: 85

δεσμωτήριον
Vol. 3: 591, 679

δεσπότης
Vol. 1: 345

δημιουργός
Vol. 1: 279, 383, 387, 389, 513, 521

δῆμος
Vol. 1: 292, 690; Vol. 2: 788f., 798; Vol. 3: 871, 1205

διάβολος
Vol. 1: 168, 449f.; Vol. 2: 381, 458; Vol. 3: 468-473, 474, 476, 628, 804, 1178

διάδημα
Vol. 1: 405

διάκονος
Vol. 1: 192, 198, 667; Vol. 2: 826; Vol. 3: 195, 544-546, 548f., 553, 596, 1065

διάλεκτος
Vol. 3: 1079

διαλογισμός
Vol. 1: 350, 566; Vol. 3: 820f., 826

διάνοια
Vol. 1: 671, 673; Vol. 2: 177, 181, 403, 493; Vol. 3: 122-125, 127f.

διδασκαλία
Vol. 2: 121, 170, 766; Vol. 3: 228, 765, 768-771

διδάσκω
Vol. 1: 191, 568, 573; Vol. 2: 36, 113, 165; Vol. 3: 44, 54, 56f., 181, 228, 509, 759-765, 769, 774, 821

δίδραχμον
Vol. 3: 752f.

διεστραμμένος
no entry

δικαιοσύνη
Vol. 1: 112, 501, 639, 701, 723; Vol. 2: 78, 245, 387f., 497, 543, 546, 595, 884; Vol. 3: 72, 92f., 161, 166, 168, 170, 184, 352-354, 358, 360--365, 369-372, 374-377, 436, 573, 575, 825f., 925, 966, 1149, 1155, 1177, 1187f.

δικαίωμα
Vol. 1: 332f., 677, 738; Vol. 3: 352, 354, 361-363, 365, 371f., 760

SYNONYM LIST

δικαίωσις
  Vol. 1: 701; Vol. 3: 352, 354, 363, 371f., 1184
δίκτυον
  no entry
δόγμα
  Vol. 1: 330f., 336, 342, 533; Vol. 2: 135, 442, 447, 453; Vol. 3: 773, 822, 877
δοκέω
  Vol. 1: 55, 330; Vol. 2: 44, 52, 393; Vol. 3: 387, 808, 821f., 826, 877
δοκιμάζω
  Vol. 3: 808-810
δολόω
  Vol. 3: 886
δόξα
  Vol. 1: 261, 327, 483, 546, 587, 594, 599, 696, 732, 735, 740; Vol. 2: 44-52, 119, 146, 162, 190, 204, 213, 242, 289f., 336, 377, 393, 482, 485, 543, 546, 563, 605, 612, 724, 781, 839; Vol. 3: 214, 257, 262, 281, 283f., 316, 344, 514, 516f., 554, 717, 723, 817, 821, 848, 925, 927, 1176, 1187, 1189
δοῦλος
  Vol. 1: 256, 283, 647, 650, 706, 709, 718, 720; Vol. 2: 254f., 508-511, 573; Vol. 3: 548, 589-591, 592-597, 599, 608-611, 613, 758, 854, 1162
δύναμις
  Vol. 1: 104, 167, 337, 398, 400; Vol. 2: 69f., 177, 388, 561, 601-606, 607-609, 615f., 654; Vol. 3: 276, 278, 281, 299, 371, 457, 711, 714, 717, 736, 927, 993, 995, 1026
δῶρον
  Vol. 2: 39-43, 120; Vol. 3: 38, 1203

E

Ἑβραῖος
  Vol. 2: 304f.; Vol. 3: 465
ἑδραῖος
  Vol. 1: 658, 660-663
ἔθνος
  Vol. 1: 541; Vol. 2: 37, 124, 127, 378, 788, 790f., 793-796, 798-801, 805, 839; Vol. 3: 38, 73, 313, 454, 567, 940, 1191, 1197
εἰκών
  Vol. 1: 95, 114, 371, 707; Vol. 2: 158, 284, 286-288, 289f., 292f., 501-503, 743; Vol. 3: 554f., 904f., 1158
εἰλικρινής
  no entry
ἐκκλησία
  Vol. 1: 10, 56, 271f., 291-293, 295-304, 306f., 490, 519, 535, 643; Vol. 2: 30, 83, 328, 349, 731, 734, 796, 805; Vol. 3: 49, 335, 384, 387, 521, 567f., 670, 675, 1141, 1194, 1201
ἔκστασις
  Vol. 1: 527f., 530; Vol. 2: 625; Vol. 3: 315
ἔλαιον
  Vol. 1: 119; Vol. 2: 710-713; Vol. 3: 869, 921f., 1162
ἔλεγχος
  Vol. 1: 713; Vol. 2: 140-142
ἐλέγχω
  Vol. 1: 89, 349; Vol. 2: 137, 140-142, 145, 768; Vol. 3: 573, 892
ἔλεος
  Vol. 1: 112; Vol. 2: 117f., 123, 449, 543f., 546, 593-597, 598f., 600; Vol. 3: 241, 889, 1201
ἕλκω
  no entry
Ἑλληνιστής
  no entry
ἐλπίς
  Vol. 1: 180, 589, 730; Vol. 2: 238-246, 545, 736, 774; Vol. 3: 214, 1151
ἔνδοξος
  no entry
ἐνέργεια
  Vol. 3: 403, 1147, 1151
ἐνθύμησις
  no entry
ἔννοια
  Vol. 3: 122f., 125, 128, 457
ἔνταλμα
  no entry
ἔντευξις
  Vol. 2: 860f.

83

SYNONYM LIST

ἐντολή
　Vol. 1: 330-337, 341f., 430; Vol. 2: 133, 177, 426f., 441, 443, 445, 451, 664, 673, 778; Vol. 3: 127, 173, 181, 239, 455, 584, 774

ἐντροπή
　no entry

ἐξουσία
　Vol. 1: 104f., 166f., 228, 301, 564, 638; Vol. 2: 161, 191, 213, 221, 561, 601, 606-611, 614, 615f., 671; Vol. 3: 97, 482, 549, 617, 645, 711, 755

ἔπαινος
　Vol. 2: 874; Vol. 3: 668, 816f.

ἐπιγινώσκω
　Vol. 2: 392, 397-399, 405; Vol. 3: 771, 808, 810

ἐπίγνωσις
　Vol. 2: 392, 397, 400f., 403, 405, 408

ἐπιείκεια
　Vol. 2: 256-259, 264

ἐπιθυμία
　Vol. 1: 106, 456-458, 460f., 645; Vol. 2: 458, 588; Vol. 3: 32, 678, 802

ἐπίσταμαι
　Vol. 3: 122

ἐπιτιμάω
　Vol. 1: 572f.; Vol. 3: 344

ἐπίτροπος
　Vol. 1: 349; Vol. 2: 254

ἐπιφάνεια
　Vol. 1: 504, 658; Vol. 2: 518, 900f.; Vol. 3: 220, 310, 316, 317-319, 505

ἐριθεία
　Vol. 1: 106, 535

ἔρις
　Vol. 1: 106, 535, 558; Vol. 2: 587; Vol. 3: 544

ἔρχομαι
　Vol. 1: 179, 319-322, 327, 358, 438, 569, 738; Vol. 2: 184, 379, 530f., 664, 758, 839, 912; Vol. 3: 181, 195, 843, 941, 998, 1173, 1181, 1212

ἐρωτάω
　Vol. 2: 855-857, 879f., 885

ἐσθίω
　Vol. 1: 253, 743f.; Vol. 2: 264, 271, 275, 277, 521, 523; Vol. 3: 793

ἕτερος
　Vol. 1: 666, 708; Vol. 2: 380, 739f., 742, 785f.; Vol. 3: 1080

εὐλάβεια
　Vol. 2: 90f.; Vol. 3: 561, 1181

εὐλαβής
　Vol. 2: 90f., 95

εὐλογέω
　Vol. 1: 206f., 212f., 217

εὐμετάδοτος
　no entry

εὐσεβής
　Vol. 2: 91-94, 596, 659

εὐτραπελία
　no entry

εὐφροσύνη
　Vol. 2: 354f., 419

εὐχαριστέω
　Vol. 1: 206, 213; Vol. 2: 855, 868, 874; Vol. 3: 675, 817-820

εὐχαριστία
　Vol. 1: 206, 213, 730; Vol. 2: 874; Vol. 3: 817-819, 820

ευχή
　Vol. 2: 861, 867

ἐχθρός
　Vol. 1: 553f., 557; Vol. 2: 742; Vol. 3: 469

Z

ζῆλος
　Vol. 1: 106, 535, 557f.; Vol. 2: 587; Vol. 3: 1166f., 1170

ζόφος
　no entry

ζωή
　Vol. 1: 337, 431, 464, 657; Vol. 2: 387f., 474, 475-483, 546, 780, 817, 928; Vol. 3: 99, 216, 309, 313, 353, 517, 832, 987, 1084, 1206, 1212

ζῶον
　Vol. 1: 640; Vol. 2: 476, 658, 689; Vol. 3: 391, 679, 684

H

ἥκω
　Vol. 1: 320f., 327

SYNONYM LIST

ἤρεμος
  no entry
ἡσύχιος
  Vol. 3: 111f.
ἥττημα
  Vol. 3: 573

Θ

θάλασσα
  Vol. 3: 982-985, 989, 992
θάμβος
  Vol. 2: 621, 623-625, 633
θαυμάσιος
  Vol. 2: 621-623
θεάομαι
  Vol. 2: 621; Vol. 3: 511f., 516
θειότης
  Vol. 2: 66, 68
θέλω
  Vol. 1: 534, 569; Vol. 2: 406; Vol. 3: 1015f., 1018-1023, 1152, 1195
θεμελιόω
  Vol. 1: 383, 660; Vol. 3: 391
θεοσεβής
  Vol. 1: 361; Vol. 2: 85, 91, 94
θεότης
  Vol. 1: 740; Vol. 2: 66, 86
θεραπεύω
  Vol. 2: 164-170; Vol. 3: 57
θεράπων
  Vol. 2: 164; Vol. 3: 609f.
θεωρέω
  Vol. 2: 393, 482; Vol. 3: 511f., 516
θηρίον
  Vol. 1: 113f., 119, 507; Vol. 2: 381, 574, 625, 653, 661, 684, 693, 776, 809, 826; Vol. 3: 256, 342, 471, 500, 715, 856, 1198
θησαυρός
  Vol. 2: 191, 829-831, 834-836, 838, 843f., 846f., 852; Vol. 3: 143, 184, 340
θιγγάνω
  no entry
θλῖψις
  Vol. 1: 741; Vol. 2: 360, 664, 766, 774, 781, 807-809, 912; Vol. 3: 956

θνητός
  Vol. 1: 430f., 435; Vol. 2: 476
θρηνέω
  Vol. 2: 416-418, 424
θρησκός
  Vol. 3: 549, 551
θρίξ
  Vol. 2: 197
θύελλα
  no entry
θυμός
  Vol. 1: 105f., 107f., 110f., 113, 456, 471; Vol. 2: 768f.; Vol. 3: 586, 676-678, 908, 1166
θύρα
  Vol. 2: 29-31, 280, 734; Vol. 3: 966
θυσία
  Vol. 2: 41f.; Vol. 3: 415, 417, 421, 428, 432f., 434f., 437, 1023
θυσιαστήριον
  Vol. 3: 417f., 428, 434f., 437, 1196

Ι

ἰάομαι
  Vol. 2: 151, 164, 166-170, 634; Vol. 3: 997f.
ἰδέα
  Vol. 2: 284, 590; Vol. 3: 224, 513
ἰδιώτης
  Vol. 2: 456f.
ἱερόν
  Vol. 2: 232-235; Vol. 3: 690, 781, 784, 785, 793, 795f., 798, 807, 812, 941, 1058
ἱεροπρεπής
  Vol. 1: 645; Vol. 2: 232f., 235
ἱερός
  Vol. 1: 243, 498, 560, 625; Vol. 2: 223f., 232-238, 324, 572, 576, 584, 644; Vol. 3: 32, 43, 478, 772, 781, 785, 1085
ἱκετηρία
  Vol. 2: 860f., 885
ἱλασμός
  Vol. 1: 89; Vol. 3: 148-151, 156, 162f.
ἱμάτιον
  Vol. 1: 312, 316f.; Vol. 2: 714

85

SYNONYM LIST

ἱματισμός
  no entry
'Ιουδαῖος
  Vol. 1: 297, 361; Vol. 2: 304f., 378, 660, 789; Vol. 3: 450
'Ισραηλίτης
  Vol. 2: 304, 310
ἰσχύς
  Vol. 1: 262, 732; Vol. 2: 177, 601f.; Vol. 3: 711, 712-714, 717

K

καθαρός
  Vol. 1: 351; Vol. 2: 144; Vol. 3: 100f., 102f., 105, 108, 167, 924, 997
καινός
  Vol. 1: 335, 384, 388f., 666; Vol. 2: 473, 524, 545, 566, 669-676, 714; Vol. 3: 168
καιρός
  Vol. 1: 268, 337, 477, 629, 722, 724, 738; Vol. 2: 37, 588, 899, 925; Vol. 3: 148, 686, 750, 826f., 831, 833-838, 841, 843f., 846-849, 954, 1041
κακία
  Vol. 1: 561, 563-565, 731; Vol. 2: 458; Vol. 3: 577, 886, 936
κακοήθεια
  no entry
κακολογέω
  Vol. 1: 206f., 413, 415, 418
κακός
  Vol. 1: 107, 125, 138, 228, 513, 561-565, 567; Vol. 3: 124, 200, 724, 1021, 1148, 1150, 1157, 1179
καλέω
  Vol. 3: 404
καλός
  Vol. 1: 197, 722; Vol. 2: 98-106; Vol. 3: 391, 770, 775, 963, 1021, 1148
καπηλεύω
  Vol. 1: 138
καταγινώσκω
  Vol. 2: 362f., 365
κατακρίνω
  Vol. 2: 362, 365

κατάλαλος
  Vol. 3: 345f.
καταλλαγή
  Vol. 1: 701; Vol. 2: 545; Vol. 3: 166-168, 581, 1112
κατάπαυσις
  Vol. 3: 73, 254f., 257f.
καταρτίζω
  Vol. 3: 349f., 1187
κατήγωρ
  Vol. 1: 82f.; Vol. 3: 470
κειρία
  no entry
κενός
  Vol. 1: 546f., 550f., 553, 671, 706f., 709; Vol. 2: 262, 343, 445, 828, 844, 854; Vol. 3: 281, 563, 604, 645
κῆνσος
  Vol. 3: 752-754
κῆπος
  no entry
κλέπτης
  Vol. 3: 377f., 381
κλίνη
  no entry
κλυδωνίζομαι
  no entry
κοινός
  Vol. 1 291f., 448, 639-642, 644; Vol. 2: 499; Vol. 3: 28, 104 1083
κοινωνικός
  Vol. 1: 639f., 642
κοινωνός
  Vol. 1: 639, 642f.; Vol. 2: 520, 661
κόλασις
  Vol. 1: 568; Vol. 3: 98f.
κόμη
  no entry
κοπιάω
  Vol. 1: 262f.; Vol. 3: 1162
κόπος
  Vol. 1: 260, 262f., 647
κόπτομαι
  Vol. 2: 417
κόσμιος
  Vol. 1: 521, 524
κόσμος
  Vol. 1: 53, 105, 377, 401, 517, 519,

SYNONYM LIST

521-526, 542, 613, 651; Vol. 2: 200, 280, 411, 420, 452, 476, 494, 511, 548, 559, 567, 609, 840; Vol. 3: 72, 168f., 217, 445, 469f., 574, 582, 789, 829, 1035, 1045, 1164, 1188, 1193

κόφινος
no entry

κράββατος
no entry

κράζω
Vol. 1: 271f., 408-410, 412; Vol. 2: 855, 873; Vol. 3: 114

κραιπάλη
Vol. 1: 514

κράτος
Vol. 2: 601, 767; Vol. 3: 711, 716-718

κραυγάζω
Vol. 1: 409

κρέας
Vol. 1: 671f., 674

κτῆμα
Vol. 2: 845

κυβεία
no entry

κύριος
Vol. 1: 71, 168, 197, 210, 212, 228, 295, 325, 469, 475, 484, 486, 571, 718; Vol. 2: 63f., 72, 80f., 155, 186, 191, 194, 203, 213, 247, 332, 338, 359, 373, 386f., 508-520, 522, 527, 530, 533, 536, 548, 562, 595, 651f., 664, 720, 735, 789, 800, 837, 867, 900f., 932; Vol. 3: 56, 115, 160, 171, 178, 221, 239, 245, 299, 341, 344, 372, 411, 484, 531, 567f., 595f., 643, 651, 709, 763, 780, 940, 1151, 1178, 1181, 1191, 1198, 1202, 1205, 1207, 1211

κῶμος
Vol. 2: 587

Λ

λαῖλαψ
Vol. 3: 1000, 1003

λαλέω
Vol. 2: 111, 113; Vol. 3: 54, 574, 1081, 1106, 1109

λαλιά
Vol. 3: 316

λαμπάς
Vol. 2: 484-486, 487

λαός
Vol. 1: 199, 299, 305, 307, 569, 732; Vol. 2: 127, 457, 788, 790f., 793, 795-801, 805, 839; Vol. 3: 161, 551, 1197

λατρεύω
Vol. 2: 94, 885; Vol. 3: 432, 544f., 549f., 553

λέγω
Vol. 1: 344, 418, 536; Vol. 2: 173, 180, 186, 281, 356, 379, 645; Vol. 3: 54, 457, 489f., 505, 822, 995, 1081f., 1087, 1106f., 1144, 1156f.

λειτουργέω
Vol. 1: 474, 544f., 549f., 551-553, 755

λῃστής
Vol. 3: 377-379, 380f.

λόγος
Vol. 1: 54, 56, 63, 107, 138, 337, 344, 397, 459, 468, 513, 546, 571, 579, 592, 636, 654, 659, 671, 736; Vol. 2: 79, 81, 113, 131, 133, 155, 158, 169f., 175, 456, 476f., 493, 518, 546, 591, 594, 643f., 657, 659, 683, 744, 766; Vol. 3: 53, 69, 122, 168f., 313, 353, 489, 540, 542, 744, 746, 765, 771f., 868, 876, 886, 941, 1026, 1031, 1036f., 1044, 1046, 1078, 1081-1087, 1106, 1108-1110, 1112, 1119-1123, 1143-1145, 1149, 1176, 1195, 1204f.

λοιδορέω
Vol. 1: 413; Vol. 3: 340f., 346f.

λούω
Vol. 1: 143f., 150-154, 160, 224, 701; Vol. 3: 180, 989, 1007

λυπέομαι
Vol. 2: 419f.

λύπη
Vol. 2: 360, 419-421, 424; Vol. 3: 725

λυτρωτής
Vol. 3: 178, 189f., 193, 199

λύχνος
Vol. 2: 484, 486f., 488, 495f.

87

SYNONYM LIST

M

μακροθυμία
Vol. 1: 646; Vol. 2: 764-771, 774, 776, 901

μαλακία
Vol. 3: 996f., 999

μαντεύομαι
Vol. 3: 74, 81

μάστιξ
Vol. 1: 161-163; Vol. 3: 996

μάταιος
Vol. 1: 546, 549-552; Vol. 2: 285, 400; Vol. 3: 200, 281, 554

μάχαιρα
Vol. 3: 958, 967

μάχη
Vol. 1:262, 644-646; Vol 2:447; Vol. 3:958f., 963

μεγαλεῖος
Vol. 2: 245

μέθη
Vol. 1: 513-515; Vol. 2: 587

μεθοδεία
Vol. 3: 935, 943

μέμφομαι
Vol. 2: 139, 143-145; Vol. 3: 932

μεριμνάω
Vol. 1: 276-278; Vol. 3: 1038

μεταμέλομαι
Vol. 1: 353-355, 356

μετανοέω
Vol. 1: 353-356, 357-359, 362, 600; Vol. 3: 103

μέτοχος
Vol. 1: 635f., 639

μετριοπαθέω
no entry

μιαίνω
Vol. 1: 447-449; Vol. 3: 925

μνημεῖον
Vol. 1: 263-265; Vol. 3: 238, 246, 268

μολύνω
Vol. 1: 448f.

μονή
Vol. 3: 224, 229

μονογενής
Vol. 1: 668; Vol. 2: 75f., 81, 723-725; Vol. 3: 1202

μορφή
Vol. 1: 50, 204, 355, 703f., 705-708, 709, 714; Vol. 2: 203, 290, 500, 673; Vol. 3: 596f., 604, 645

μόχθος
Vol. 1: 262

μῦθος
Vol. 2: 613, 643-645, 647; Vol. 3: 274, 1033, 1081

μυκάομαι
no entry

μύρον
Vol. 1: 119, 124; Vol. 2: 294f., 712

μώλωψ
Vol. 1: 163f.

μωρία
Vol. 2: 143, 619, 709; Vol. 3: 53, 1023, 1025f.

μωρολογία
Vol. 3: 1026

N

ναός
Vol. 1: 234; Vol. 2: 233, 235f., 250; Vol. 3: 185, 781-785, 789, 792f., 796f.

νεκρός
Vol. 1: 429, 436, 443-446; Vol. 2: 554; Vol. 3: 268, 278, 299, 303, 1176, 1189, 1207f.

νέος
Vol. 2: 669-671, 674-676, 714; Vol. 3: 457, 785

νεφέλη
Vol. 2: 912; Vol. 3: 1000, 1003

νέφος
Vol. 3: 1003

νίπτω
Vol. 1: 143f., 150-152, 153f., 160, 224f.; Vol. 2: 144, 150

νομικός
Vol. 2: 438, 443, 447; Vol. 3: 353, 409, 477, 480

νομοδιδάσκαλος
Vol. 2: 438, 447; Vol. 3: 477, 480, 765, 768

SYNONYM LIST

νόμος
Vol. 1: 54, 94, 228, 245, 282, 334, 336f., 715, 738; Vol. 2: 120, 131, 436f., 437-450, 452, 455, 519, 540f., 544, 546, 658f., 662, 715; Vol. 3: 72, 181, 185f., 239, 353f., 480, 493, 573f., 580, 583f., 593, 596f., 885, 1151, 1178, 1188

νόσος
Vol. 3: 993f., 996-999, 1000, 1119

νουθεσία
Vol. 1: 568f.

νουθετέω
Vol. 1: 329, 567f., 573

νοῦς
Vol. 1: 232, 355-357, 443f., 481, 521, 546, 557, 568, 595, 636, 638, 671, 676, 693, 706, 708, 739; Vol. 2: 182, 212, 439, 476, 493, 564f., 567, 590f.; Vol. 3: 122-130, 153, 224, 351, 572, 672, 678, 681, 689, 809, 936, 939, 1198

νῦν
Vol. 2: 282, 329, 416, 480, 543, 912; Vol. 3: 826, 831, 833f., 837, 841, 843, 850, 1169

νωθρός
no entry

Ξ

ξένος
Vol. 1: 683, 686-689, 691; Vol. 2: 99, 538, 742, 794, 803

ξύλον
Vol. 1: 214, 389f., 394, 404; Vol. 3: 391, 865f., 868, 870, 1195f.

Ο

ὄγκος
Vol. 1: 671, 674

ὀδύνη
Vol. 1: 726; Vol. 2: 419; Vol. 3: 229

ὀθόνη
no entry

οἶδα
Vol. 2: 391f., 398, 719; Vol. 3: 1064, 1205

οἰκέτης
Vol. 2: 509; Vol. 3: 609

οἰκία
Vol. 2: 247f., 250

οἰκονόμος
Vol. 2: 253-255

οἶκος
Vol. 1: 149, 197, 300, 662, 690; Vol. 2: 129, 247-256, 873; Vol. 3: 229, 465, 504, 593, 782, 794, 1201

οἰκτιρμός
Vol. 2: 116, 543, 593, 594, 597, 598, 599f., 733

οἰνοφλυγία
Vol. 1: 514; Vol. 3: 918, 922

ὄλεθρος
Vol. 1: 462, 464, 465-467, 500; Vol. 2: 33, 368; Vol. 3: 97, 214, 471, 477, 535, 537

ὁλόκληρος
no entry

ὄμβρος
Vol. 3: 1000, 1003

ὄμμα
Vol. 2: 393; Vol. 3: 512

ὁμοίωμα
Vol. 2: 284, 500-504; Vol. 3: 904

ὁμοίωσις
Vol. 2: 500-502, 505, 743

ὀνειδίζω
Vol. 2: 835; Vol. 3: 257, 340f.

ὀνομάζω
Vol. 2: 648, 655; Vol. 3: 233, 341

ὀπτάνομαι
Vol. 3: 516, 1181

ὁράω
Vol. 1: 695; Vol. 2: 134, 173, 176, 180, 555, 768; Vol. 3: 281, 284f., 509, 511-513, 515f., 521, 1046, 1206

ὀργή
Vol. 1: 106-108, 110--113, 464; Vol. 2: 412, 544, 834, 924; Vol. 3: 205, 315, 580, 836, 1166, 1187

ὄρεξις
Vol. 1: 460f.; Vol. 3: 587

89

SYNONYM LIST

ὁρμή
Vol. 1: 710

ὄρνεν
Vol. 2: 591; Vol. 3: 1009, 1013f., 1094

ὄρος
no entry

ὅσιος
Vol. 2: 93, 223, 232, 236-238

ὀφειλή
Vol. 2: 666, 668; Vol. 3: 754

ὀφθαλμός
Vol. 2: 710, 925; Vol. 3: 32, 511f., 516, 1179

ὄχλος
Vol. 1: 292f.; Vol. 2: 448, 788f., 796, 799, 800f., 805

Π

πάθος
Vol. 1: 108, 674; Vol. 2: 419, 658

παιδάριον
Vol. 1: 283f.; Vol. 2: 428

παιδεία
Vol. 1: 462, 568f., 639; Vol. 2: 140f., 745; Vol. 3: 311, 688, 745, 775-777, 779, 998

παιδίον
Vol. 1: 280, 283-285; Vol. 3: 352

παιδίσκη
Vol. 1: 283f.

παῖς
Vol. 1: 96, 273, 280f., 283f., 286, 290, 538, 552, 597, 707; Vol. 2: 151, 229, 337, 364, 643; Vol. 3: 590, 593, 607-612, 634f., 637, 640, 664, 721, 775

παῖς θεοῦ
Vol. 1: 281, 283, 538; Vol. 3: 597, 607, 610-612, 634f., 640, 664, 721

παλαιός
Vol. 1: 192, 339, 401, 666, 671, 682; Vol. 2: 473, 566, 669, 675f., 713f., 716

παλιγγενεσία
Vol. 1: 176, 178, 180, 184f., 188, 290, 521; Vol. 2: 566, 625, 673, 836; Vol. 3: 215, 220, 629

πανήγυρις
Vol. 1: 304

πανουργία
Vol. 1: 412f.

παράβασις
Vol. 1: 85; Vol. 3: 573f., 583-585

παραβολή
Vol. 1: 577; Vol. 2: 502, 743f., 746, 748, 753, 757f., 803; Vol. 3: 131, 503, 555, 906, 1014, 1070, 1106

παραγγελία
Vol. 1: 340f.

παράδεισος
Vol. 2: 760f., 764; Vol. 3: 315, 602

παράδοξος
no entry

παράκλησις
Vol. 1: 329, 569-571; Vol. 2: 121, 766, 774; Vol. 3: 87f., 751

παρακοή
Vol. 2: 172, 175; Vol. 3: 573, 585

παραλογίζομαι
Vol. 2: 457-459

παραμυθία
Vol. 1: 328f.

παρανομία
no entry

παράπτωμα
Vol. 1: 446, 606, 608, 701; Vol. 2: 120, 586; Vol. 3: 168, 573, 585f., 1176, 1184

παρεπίδημος
Vol. 1: 305, 683, 689, 690, 691; Vol. 2: 788-790, 794, 803

πάρεσις
Vol. 1: 573, 697f., 701f.; Vol. 2: 767; Vol. 3: 1184

παρηγορία
no entry

πάροικος
Vol. 1: 683f., 686-689, 690f.; Vol. 2: 249, 251

παροιμία
Vol. 2: 736, 743, 745, 756f., 760

παροργισμός
Vol. 2: 107, 110

πατρία
Vol. 1: 615f., 621; Vol. 2: 655f.

SYNONYM LIST

πέδη
no entry
πειράζω
Vol. 3: 790, 798f., 801f., 808-810, 1198
πέλαγος
no entry
πέμπω
Vol. 1: 126-128
πένης
Vol. 2: 257, 264, 820-822, 828
πενθέω
Vol. 2: 416-418, 420, 421-423
περιφέρω
Vol. 3: 770
πετεινόν
Vol. 1: 172; Vol. 2: 729
πηγή
Vol. 3: 982, 985-987, 988-990
πηλός
Vol. 3: 911, 915f.
πικρία
Vol. 1: 106, 202, 726
πλανάω
Vol. 1: 608; Vol. 2: 457-461, 469
πλεονεξία
Vol. 1: 137-139, 214; Vol. 2: 286, 845f.
πληγή
Vol. 1: 161-163; Vol. 3: 857
πληρόω
Vol. 1: 93, 171, 532, 552, 728, 733-738, 740, 741, 744; Vol. 2: 77, 83, 87, 251, 359, 417, 629, 640, 669, 715, 753, 819; Vol. 3: 53, 71, 82, 172, 181f., 187, 329, 489, 491, 494, 505, 642, 804, 827, 1073, 1121
πλύνω
Vol. 1: 150, 152f.

πνεῦμα
Vol. 1: 66, 90, 232, 234-236, 449, 452, 470, 500f., 637, 674f., 719, 739; Vol. 2: 213, 233, 242, 388, 476, 479, 520, 546, 559, 617, 641, 672f., 675, 691, 715, 784, 824, 878, 899, 919; Vol. 3: 75, 129, 257f., 299, 471, 473, 475, 493, 495, 597, 672, 678, 680f., 685, 689f., 693-695, 700, 706, 708f.,
711, 831, 967, 1046, 1172, 1177f., 1183, 1188-1192, 1199f., 1202f., 1210
πνοή
Vol. 3: 680, 689, 707
ποδήρης
no entry
ποιέω
Vol. 1: 363, 377f., 380, 383, 387, 590, 722; Vol. 2: 100, 221, 597, 664, 709; Vol. 3: 148f., 168, 170, 242f., 245, 316, 353, 372, 719, 859, 1021f., 1083, 1148f., 1152-1158
ποιμαίνω
Vol. 1: 408; Vol. 3: 464, 566, 568
πόλεμος
Vol. 1: 644f., 652; Vol. 3: 958f., 961-963, 981
πονηρός
Vol. 1: 228, 348, 561-563, 564-567, 656, 722; Vol. 2: 103, 351, 584, 868; Vol. 3: 124, 204, 469f., 473, 475, 572, 579, 1148, 1150, 1176
πόνος
Vol. 1: 260, 262, 271, 459, 564, 647; Vol. 2: 820
ποταμός
Vol. 3: 982, 985, 987, 989f., 992
πότος
Vol. 2: 274
πραότης
praytes Vol. 2: 256-259, 263, 771
πράσσω
Vol. 3: 719, 1148, 1150, 1155-1159
πραΰς
Vol. 2: 201, 256-264, 771, 822; Vol. 3: 218, 807, 1032
πρεσβύτης
Vol. 1: 192f., 197, 536
προσευχή
Vol. 2: 530, 860, 861, 863, 867, 875
προσφορά
Vol. 2: 40-42; Vol. 3: 38, 417, 431-434
προφητεύω
Vol. 1: 527, 529; Vol. 2: 443; Vol. 3: 74-76, 87, 533

SYNONYM LIST

πρωτότοκος
  Vol. 1: 288, 304, 445, 664-666, 667-669; Vol. 2: 157, 725, 729; Vol. 3: 38, 416
πτόησις
  no entry
πτωχός
  Vol. 2: 110, 257, 264, 453, 820, 821-824, 828, 834, 843f., 846, 852; Vol. 3: 70, 119, 241, 351, 499, 525, 545f., 548, 553, 572, 727, 752, 810
πύλη
  Vol. 2: 29-31
πυνθάνομαι
  no entry

Ρ

ῥῆμα
  Vol. 3: 749, 967, 1078, 1081, 1087, 1106f., 1113f., 1119-1122, 1143-1145
ῥιζούμαι
  Vol. 1: 660; see rhizoo Vol. 3: 865, 868
ῥομφαία
  Vol. 2: 686; Vol. 3: 959, 967

Σ

σαγήνη
  no entry
σαρκικός
  Vol. 1: 671, 677, 682, 764; Vol. 2: 120; Vol. 3: 963, 1200
σάρκινος
  Vol. 1: 236, 337, 671, 674, 682
σάρξ
  Vol. 1: 188, 221f., 228, 233, 236, 257, 446, 457, 461, 535, 592, 647, 671f., 674-682, 719; Vol. 2: 242, 273, 349, 477, 504, 525, 535, 566, 579, 589, 617, 816, 919; Vol. 3: 32, 54, 171, 227, 313, 322f., 581, 587, 724, 811, 994, 1073, 1115, 1117, 1151, 1158, 1172, 1175f., 1188, 1195f., 1199f.
σεμνός
  Vol. 2: 91-93, 232; Vol. 3: 727
σημεῖον
  Vol. 2: 192, 350, 352, 621, 625, 626f., 629, 633f., 858
σιγάω
  no entry
σικάριος
  no entry
σιωπάω
  no entry
σκληρός
  Vol. 2: 153-156
σκολιός
  no entry
σκότος
  Vol. 1: 301, 420f., 423, 425; Vol. 2; 484, 490, 543; Vol. 3: 554, 831, 1151
σοφία
  Vol. 1: 165, 228, 400, 485, 501, 592, 692, 696; Vol. 2: 61, 99, 120, 127, 355, 406, 493, 616, 620; Vol. 3: 53, 68, 76, 129f., 678, 765, 898, 925, 1026--1028, 1030--1032, 1033, 1036f., 1144
σπαταλάω
  no entry
σπυρίς
  no entry
σταυρός
  Vol. 1: 197, 228, 389, 391-399, 403f., 437, 726; Vol. 2: 139, 379; Vol. 3: 172, 641, 1026, 1199
στενοχωρία
  Vol. 2: 807f.
στέφανος
  Vol. 1: 405f.
στηρίζω
  Vol. 1: 660; Vol. 3: 87
στίγμα
  Vol. 1: 235; Vol. 2: 572, 574, 575
στολή
  Vol. 1: 312, 317
στρηνιάω
  no entry
συλλαμβάνω
  Vol. 1: 187, 343f.

SYNONYM LIST

συμπαθέω
  Vol. 3: 719, 722, 724
συναγωγή
  Vol. 1: 69, 245, 272, 291-293, 295-297, 307, 589; Vol. 3: 479, 868
σύρω
  no entry
σχῆμα
  Vol. 1: 703, 707, 708f., 714; Vol. 2: 203, 500, 673; Vol. 3: 564, 604, 864
σχίσμα
  Vol. 1: 535; Vol. 3: 543f.
σωτήρ
  Vol. 1: 519; Vol. 2: 78, 158, 332, 349, 584; Vol. 3: 71, 177, 205, 210, 216-223, 318, 462, 1022, 1046
σωφρονίζω
  no entry
σωφροσύνη
  Vol. 1: 494, 501f., 529, 550; Vol. 3: 27, 354, 561f., 925

T

ταμιεῖον
  no entry
ταπεινοφροσύνη
  Vol. 2: 259-264, 617; Vol. 3: 928
ταράσσω
  Vol. 3: 709f.
ταρτάρος
  no entry
τάφος
  Vol. 1: 263-265; Vol. 2: 727
τεθεμελεωμένος
  see themelioo Vol. 1: 383, 660; Vol. 3: 391
τέκνον
  Vol. 1: 256, 280, 284-287, 290f., 416; Vol. 3: 607, 647
τέλειος
  Vol. 1: 92, 649; Vol. 2: 59-65, 77, 162, 449, 477, 563, 741, 778, 782; Vol. 3: 350, 502, 504, 1021, 1031
τελειόω
  Vol. 2: 59-66; Vol. 3: 491, 756
τέλος
  Vol. 1: 69, 164, 429, 741; Vol. 2: 52, 58, 59-66, 157, 445, 713, 715, 741, 904; Vol. 3: 277, 363, 725, 752, 754-756, 759, 779, 838, 924
τελώνης
  Vol. 3: 755, 757, 759
τέρας
  Vol. 2: 621, 626f., 629, 633f.
τεχνίτης
  Vol. 1: 279, 387
τηρέω
  Vol. 1: 336f.; Vol. 2: 132f., 135, 137
τιμή
  Vol. 1: 222; Vol. 2: 44, 47-50, 52; Vol. 3: 138, 174, 198, 200, 717, 817
τιμωρία
  no entry
τρυφάω
  no entry
τρώγω
  Vol. 2: 535f.
τύπος
  Vol. 1: 71, 86, 371, 491, 744; Vol. 2: 277, 284, 290, 760; Vol. 3: 61, 555, 903-907, 1015
τυρβάζω
  no entry

Y

ὑβριστής
  Vol. 3: 27-29, 31
ὑετός
  Vol. 3: 1000, 1003
υἱός
  Vol. 1: 181, 256, 280f., 284, 286-290, 487, 523, 595, 615, 619, 667f.; Vol. 2: 81, 194, 216, 324, 337, 374, 376, 380, 385, 387, 502f., 514, 565, 585, 607, 630, 656, 725, 900, 912; Vol. 3: 147, 195, 299, 530, 597, 607, 609, 611-613, 617, 620, 630, 634f., 639, 641, 648, 651, 658, 665f., 751, 831, 1085, 1144, 1202
υἱὸς θεοῦ
  Vol. 1: 281, 615; Vol. 3: 299, 607, 611, 634, 651, 1085
ὕμνος
  Vol. 1: 213; Vol. 2: 874; Vol. 3: 668-670, 672, 674f., 816

SYNONYM LIST

ὑπάρξεις
Vol. 1: 711; Vol. 2: 829, 844, 845-847
ὑπεναντίος
no entry
ὑπέρ
Vol. 1: 197, 227, 398, 647, 728f.; Vol. 2: 486, 523f., 543, 587, 617, 819; Vol. 3: 153, 168, 170, 195, 197, 611, 1171-1174, 1176, 1180, 1193, 1196f., 1199, 1203, 1207f., 1214
ὑπερήφανος
Vol. 3: 27-32, 127
ὑπηρέτης
Vol. 3: 544, 546, 609
ὑπογραμμός
Vol. 2: 291; Vol. 3: 724, 905
ὑπόδειγμα
Vol. 2: 284, 290, 293; Vol. 3: 555, 570, 905
ὑπόμνησις
Vol. 3: 230, 241-243, 247
ὑπομονή
Vol. 1: 646; Vol. 2: 243, 245, 772-776, 782, 809; Vol. 3: 73, 555
ὑποτύπωσις
Vol. 3: 903-905
ὗς
Vol. 1: 117

Φ

φάγομαι
See φαίνω Vol. 2: 433, 484, 487f., 496; Vol. 3: 310, 312, 317, 320
φαίνομαι
Vol. 2: 484, 487f.; Vol. 3: 310
φανέρωσις
Vol. 3: 317, 323
φαῦλος
Vol. 1: 561, 564; Vol. 3: 1158
φέγγος
Vol. 2: 484
φέρω
Vol. 1: 722; Vol. 3: 1195
φθόνος
Vol. 1: 557f.
φιλαργυρία
Vol. 1: 138; Vol. 2: 550, 845

φίλαυτος
Vol. 2: 550
φιλέω
Vol. 1: 206; Vol. 2: 86, 538f., 542f., 547-551, 585
φόβος
Vol. 1: 621f.; Vol. 2: 93f., 396; Vol. 3: 561, 721
φονεύς
no entry
φορέω
no entry
φόρος
Vol. 3: 752, 754
φορτίον
Vol. 1: 260f., 335; Vol. 3: 1162
φρέαρ
Vol. 3: 986
φρόνησις
Vol. 1: 485; Vol. 2: 616f., 620; Vol. 3: 354, 898, 1032
φροντίζω
Vol. 1: 276f.; Vol. 3: 823
φρουρέω
Vol. 2: 134f.
φυλακή
Vol. 2: 134, 136, 207
φυλάσσω
Vol. 2: 132f., 134f., 137, 177, 450, 452, 864
φυλή
Vol. 1: 518, 684; Vol. 2: 306; Vol. 3: 870f., 873
φωνή
Vol. 2: 426; Vol. 3: 51, 80, 113f., 394, 675, 1078, 1143
φῶς
Vol. 1: 421-424, 723; Vol. 2: 290, 397, 477, 480, 484-487, 490, 493, 496; Vol. 3: 312f., 317, 554, 734
φωστήρ
Vol. 2: 490, 493

X

χαρά
Vol. 1: 400, 459f., 731, 741; Vol. 2:

SYNONYM LIST

115, 355, 356-359, 388, 420, 423, 431, 433; Vol. 3: 1180
χάρις
  Vol. 1: 52, 112, 247, 300, 571, 601, 739; Vol. 2: 115-124, 131, 356, 360, 543, 546, 614, 780; Vol. 3: 252, 717, 746, 817, 854, 889, 1151, 1179
χείμαρρος
  no entry
χιτών
  no entry
χλαμύς
  no entry
χοῖρος
  Vol. 1: 117
χολή
  Vol. 2: 27f.
χρηστότης
  Vol. 2: 105-107, 766, 770f; Vol. 3: 227
χρίω
  Vol. 1: 53, 119-123; Vol. 2: 334f., 347, 711; Vol. 3: 499, 1060
χρόνος
  Vol. 1: 326, 734, 738; Vol. 3: 148, 826f., 833-835, 839-844
χωρίς
  Vol. 2: 446

Ψ

ψαλμός
  Vol. 2: 874; Vol. 3: 668, 670f., 674f.
ψευδόχριστος
  Vol. 1: 124f.; Vol. 2: 472
ψηλαφάω
  no entry
ψιθυριστής
  Vol. 3: 346
ψυχικός
  Vol. 1: 236; Vol. 2: 567; Vol. 3: 281, 301, 504, 676, 684, 686f.

Ω

ᾠδή
  Vol. 2: 874; Vol. 3: 668, 670f., 672-675, 676
ὠδίν
  Vol. 3: 180, 857-859
ὡραῖος
  Vol. 3: 845, 847
ὠρύομαι
  no entry